INSIDE MONTGOMERY BUS BOYCOTT

MY PERSONAL STORY

URIAH J. FIELDS, M.Div., Ph.D.

AmErica House
Baltimore

First printing

ISBN: 1-58851-634-2
The Library of Congress Control Number – 2001 130993
PUBLISHED BY AMERICA HOUSE BOOK PUBLISHERS
www.publishamerica.com
Baltimore

Printed in the United States of America

For Our Children
and in Memory of Our Ancestors

BE IT KNOWN BY ALL THAT NIXON IS THE ONE!

Edgar Daniel Nixon, more than any other single person, is the one who called the people of Montgomery, not to arms, but to feet to walk, to not ride buses, and inspired them to continue to not ride them until after the Supreme Court's decision declared that segregation on Montgomery buses was unconstitutional.

It is true that Rosa Parks refused to give up her bus seat to a white man, that Martin Luther King, Jr. was unquestionably the chief leader of the Montgomery bus protest, that Ralph Abernathy, Jo Ann Robinson, A. W. Wilson, Fred Gray, S. S. Seay, Robert Graetz, Charles Langford, Rufus Lewis, myself and other leaders performed a yeoman's job, that bus boycotters, black people and a few white people in Montgomery that included Clifford and Virginia Durr, that many people of good will from throughout America contributed admirably, financially and morally, to support the bus boycott, it remains a historical fact that cannot be denied by anyone considering the facts that E. D. Nixon, the unsung hero of the Montgomery Bus Boycott, deserves "credit par excellence" for being the person who rallied black Montgomerians to boycott buses and inspired them more than anyone to continue the boycott of buses in Montgomery for 382 days and until they were desegregated.

LORD, FORGIVE ME WHEN I WHINE!

Today upon a bus, I saw a lovely girl with golden hair,

I envied her she seemed so gay and I wished I were as fair.

When suddenly she rose to leave, I saw her hobble down the aisle;
She had one leg and wore a crutch; But as she passed a smile!

Oh God forgive me when I whine, I have two legs. The world is mine!

I stopped to buy some candy. The lad who sold it had such charm.

I talked with him. He seemed so glad. If I were late 'twould do no harm,
And as I left he said to me, "I thank you. You have been so kind.
It's nice to talk with folk like you." You see, he said, "I'm blind."
Oh, God forgive me when I whine, I have two eyes. The world is mine!

Later while walking down the street I saw a child with eyes of blue.
He stood and watched the others play. He did not know what to do.
I stopped a moment, then I said, "Why don't you join the others dear?"
He looked ahead without a word, and then I knew he could not hear.
Oh, God forgive me when I whine, I have two ears. The world is mine!

With feet to take me where I'd go, with eyes to see the sunset's glow,
with ears to hear what I would know, Oh God forgive me when I whine. I'm blessed indeed. The world is mine!

– Anonymous

Table of Contents

INTRODUCTION

"Why another book about the Montgomery Bus Boycott?" This is a valid question to be asked, especially by people who have read books written about the Montgomery Bus Boycott and, even more importantly, by anyone who may be considering writing a book on this subject. Since the publication of the first book on the Montgomery Bus Boycott in 1958, "Stride Toward Freedom," by Martin Luther King, Jr., there have been a number of books written about the Montgomery Bus Boycott. Some of them have been partly factual and informative but most of them have been fantasy stories or, more correctly, fables about the Montgomery Bus Boycott. In a word, they all have told lies about the bus boycott. All of them, without exception, have omitted valuable information and contained significant inaccuracies about the bus boycott. Conflicting stories about the Montgomery movement have made it difficult for people who wanted to know and had a right to know the truth about the bus boycott to obtain it. Fiction has been presented as nonfiction.

Having said that, and I realize that I have made a strong charge, I want to acknowledge that there are three books on the list of books about the Montgomery Bus Boycott that are highly factual, although the authors of these books could not bring to their writings the vital quality that was available to an insider. An outsider who did not participate in the bus boycott cannot be a witness to the bus boycott. An insider who participated in the bus boycott helped to make the history that the outsider can only write about. The three books I consider to be substantive and meritorious are: "Bearing the Cross" (1986), by David J. Garrow, "Parting the Waters" (1988), by Taylor C. Branch and "The Papers of Martin Luther King, Jr., Vol. III" (1997), by Senior Editor Clayborne Carson.

Because I have said that all the books written about the Montgomery Bus Boycott, without exception, have omitted valuable information and contain inaccuracies and, in some cases, told lies, I want to speak briefly to this point. Someone asked me, "Did King lie in his book?" I replied forthrightly, "He did not tell the truth about me in his first book on the Montgomery Bus Boycott." His wife, Coretta Scott King, in her book, "My Life with Martin Luther King, Jr." (1969), listed the names of all the officers of the Montgomery Improvement Association except mine. Apparently, her resentment for me was the reason why she refused to include my name as an officer of the Montgomery Improvement Association, even though I was a founder and the original secretary of the organization during the first six months of the bus boycott. By her deliberate omission of my name she failed to tell the truth. She certainly did not tell the whole truth, not the truth that she knew. Years later when she came to Los Angeles, where I was a resident, for the dedication of the Martin Luther King, Jr. Hospital in that city she snubbed me, although she had embraced me in her own home shortly after her first child Yolanda was born.

In light of these inaccuracies, fallacies and, in some instances, lies, about the Montgomery movement there is a definite need for someone to write a true story about the Montgomery Bus Boycott. For more than forty years I had hoped that someone would write such a book, but nobody did. I asked myself: "If a book telling the true story of the Montgomery Bus Boycott is to be written, Why don't I write it?" The answer I received was: "You, an insider of the Montgomery movement, are the person best qualified to write this true story about the Montgomery movement." I then abandoned any thought that I had about waiting for someone else to write a true story about the bus boycott and became passionately committed to writing this book.

I am an insider of the Montgomery Bus Boycott. With Martin Luther King, Jr., E. D. Nixon, Ralph David Abernathy and fourteen other persons we founded the Montgomery Improvement Association, four days after Rosa Parks was arrested for having violated the segregation laws of Alabama when she sat in a seat that was in the "white only" section of a Montgomery bus. During that organizing meeting King was elected president and I was elected recording secretary of the Montgomery Improvement Association. The MIA was formed to provide organizational leadership for the Montgomery Bus Boycott. While serving as the secretary of the MIA the first half of the one year, two weeks and three-day old bus boycott I did not only record the minutes of the MIA executive board meetings and handled some of the organization's correspondence, but I helped to make decisions and develop strategies that were employed in conducting the bus boycott. My first-hand experience, derived from my active participation as a leader of the bus boycott, enables me to include information in my book that other writers on this subject were not privy to. Only an insider who was intimately involved with other bus boycott leaders could know about the true dynamics and the feelings of leaders that were expressed when they were behind closed doors, in board meetings, and when they shared their reflections with each other, acknowledged their pain and admitted their fears and doubts, particularly their fear that the bus boycott may end without accomplishing anything significant for black people in Montgomery, many of whom had made sacrifices and suffered severely for their involvement in the bus boycott.

I recall that fear mixed with disenchantment and a feeling of betrayal were in bold evidence when the executive board met on Monday, January 23, 1956, following the weekend when three black ministers had met with the Mayor of Montgomery and some other white city officials. Following the meeting a spokesman for the mayor informed the news media that black people had called off the bus boycott and would be resuming riding the buses on Monday. Of course, these self-appointed black ministers were not leaders of the bus boycott. Nevertheless, the fallout from this media story had been damaging and emotionally draining on boycott leaders. I had never seen King as visibly shaken and distraught as he was on that day. He offered his resignation to the MIA executive board. The members of the executive board pleaded with him to remain as the president of the MIA and chief leader of the Montgomery movement. Reverend S. S. Seay, a senior and respected minister, said tearfully to King, "You are young and well-trained in the spirit. I will drink my portion of the cup, but you can drink of it deeper." Reverend A. W. Wilson, pastor of the Holt Street Baptist Church where the first bus boycott mass meeting had been held not quite eight weeks earlier, said, "Brother King, I would like to see the bus boycott continue, but most people feel as I do, that without your leadership we should call off the bus boycott immediately." The executive board gave King a unanimous vote of confidence. Seemingly, reluctantly and dreadfully, King withdrew his resignation and continued to serve as the president of the MIA and as the chief leader of the bus boycott. During the remaining months of the boycott there would be many incidents that would bring pain and anguish to King and other leaders of the bus boycott. Of course, King would suffer the most.

The question that might be asked this writer is: "Why have you waited these many years to write this book?" Frankly, I had hoped that someone else would write a true story about the Montgomery Bus Boycott. About a year after King's book, "Stride Toward Freedom" was published my book, "The Montgomery Story: The Unhappy Effects of the Montgomery Bus Boycott" was published. But because I had been so greatly disenchanted with some bus boycott leaders, displeased with how I had been treated by them, painfully wounded and vengeance-ridden, admittedly, I was in no condition to write objectively and compassionately about the Montgomery Bus Boycott. In that book I presented a mostly bitter story about the Montgomery Bus Boycott because I was bitter. Some twenty years later, after I had forgiven, "seven times seven," everyone who I had held a grudge against or resented, I gave serious thought to writing an objective story about the Montgomery Bus Boycott, but for a number of years my work as a minister, educator and social psychologist consumed nearly all of my waking hours, leaving me little time for writing. So I abandoned any thought of writing a book about the bus boycott, however, I never ceased to think about the need for someone to write a truth book about the Montgomery Bus Boycott. Whenever I read a new book about the bus boycott, filled with half-truths or less, as was usually the case, I became somewhat infuriated and enraged. At such times a feeling welled-up within me that caused me to give additional consideration to writing a book that would give a true account of the Montgomery Bus Boycott. I also realized that if it was not too late for people to write about President Abraham Lincoln, then it was not too late for me to write about the Montgomery Bus Boycott.

Now that I have reached the september years of my life and no longer am limited by earlier strictures or under the restraints that previously existed when I was engaged professionally in my work, I am willing, ready, and highly motivated to write a truth book about the Montgomery Bus Boycott. It takes time to tell the truth just as it takes time to live the truth that one writes about. It takes time to write a book about the Montgomery Bus Boycott.

On my honor I swear upon the altar of all eternity and solemnly promise to tell the truth, nothing but the truth, and the whole truth, in this book, as much as it is possible for me to do so, about the Montgomery Bus Boycott. I promise to tell a fuller truth about the Montgomery Bus Boycott than anyone has done before and to do it with brevity and without the inclusion of erroneous materials and with a bare minimum of hearsay evidence. I am a witness who was involved in the leadership of the Montgomery Bus Boycott. I was there. I experienced first-hand the bus boycott.

I bear on my body battlefield scars and within my soul indelible, maybe eternal, pain; a portion of which came from soul-searching that, in a certain way, has turned into joy that can come only from the excruciating pain such as I experienced while fighting to bring justice to black bus riders in Montgomery and hopefully to other victims of injustice who reside in other places and even at other times. I proudly answer the summon issued by my conscience and the plea made by those who want to know the truth about the Montgomery Bus Boycott. I willingly and gladly testify about the things that I have seen, felt and learned from my Montgomery Bus Boycott experience. Here, I will state my case of which I am certain. In this presentation and evaluation of my testimony I do not need any validation other than self-validation.

This book chronicles the events that characterize the Montgomery Bus Boycott and presents people who were involved in directing and promoting the bus boycott. The dynamics and spirit-states of bus boycott leaders and some other participants in the Montgomery movement are viewed by me from close-up and I give an eye-witness and uncensored account of what I perceived and experienced on the pages ahead.

In the "Introduction," as the reader has probably already observed, I indicate why it was necessary for me to write this book, emphasizing my commitment to correct some of the untrues that some other writers have told in giving fictionalized accounts of the bus boycott. I discuss the nature of the relationship that I had with King and other bus boycott leaders, and the role I assumed in helping to conduct the bus boycott.

In the "Introduction" I also let the reader know what he can expect from reading this chronological account of the Montgomery Bus Boycott.

Part One focuses on my life in Montgomery during the three years immediately prior to the Montgomery Bus Boycott, including my matriculation at Alabama State College in Montgomery where I was president of the Student College Council, my persistent fight to become a registered voter in Alabama, my pastoral leadership of a church for two years prior to the bus boycott and my association and work with E. D. Nixon who, at the time, was the chief black leader of Montgomery.

Part Two discusses in a journal-like fashion the first half of the twelve-month long Montgomery Bus Boycott: the significant occurrences, and players, including those who were for and those who were against the bus boycott, the ordeal experienced by black people in Montgomery, the violence that was generated, primarily by the White Citizens Council and the Montgomery police, the unwavering resolve of black people to continue the bus boycott in the face of strong opposition and suffering, and the sustained financial and moral support received from black and white people throughout America.

Part Three covers the last half of the bus boycott. It begins with me resigning as the secretary of the Montgomery Improvement Association and severing my relationship with most bus boycott leaders. It also depicts the events and incidents that occurred during the last half of the bus boycott and the significant actions taken by boycott leaders and some other personalities. This section of the book ends with a discussion on the United States Supreme Court's decision that banned segregation on buses in Montgomery.

Part Four focuses on black people's decision to end a 382-day long bus boycott and return to riding Montgomery buses following the U.S. Supreme Court's decision outlawing segregation on Montgomery buses. Also discussed is the violence and bombing that occurred after the buses were integrated, including the bombing of four churches and two parsonages in six locations in the wee hours of the morning of January 10, 1957.

The "Epilogue" presents "The Legacy of Martin Luther King, Jr."

Both the negative and positive aspects of his legacy are presented. King is recognized as being the leader who contributed most to the advancement of black people in America. His leadership is credited with having made it possible for black people to gain access to desegregated public facilities, to voting in the South, open housing and forcing change in the practices and laws that had excluded black people from enjoying many of the rights that were enjoyed by white Americans.

I invite the reader of this volume to come "inside," i.e., read this "insider's" account of the Montgomery Bus Boycott and acquire a new perspective on this historical event, one that can only be gained from reading an insider's account of the bus boycott. It bears repeating, no outsider has been privy to significant information or had the on-site experience that would enable him to tell the true story about the bus boycott as you will glean from the pages ahead. Ultimately, the Montgomery Story is a love story that reveals how love redeemed a city and pricked the conscience of a nation.

PART ONE

My Life in Montgomery Before the Montgomery Bus Boycott

While serving in the military I vowed to never return to live in the South. Prior to enlisting in the United States Army I had, just shy by a few days, lived all my eighteen years in my native state of Alabama. I had grown up with segregation which I hated, but after experiencing integration in the Army, despite the fact that I served a third of my enlistment time in segregated units, and in the North I detested segregation even more. About a year after I was in the Army I began to say to myself: "No more going to the back of the bus; no more being denied the right to go to a public restaurant, movie theater, restroom," and on and on my litany of "no-more" embracing segregation practices resounded. Experiencing integration had increased my self-esteem, given me a heightened sense of dignity and caused me to feel freer than I had remembered feeling before.

No, I was not so naive as to think that I had escaped entirely from the clutches of segregation and racial discrimination. Indeed, I experienced segregation and racial discrimination in some form or fashion in the Army and the North. But because segregation was not legalized in the North and was practiced in a less rigid manner in the Army than in the South, I felt that I had a reprieve from the sentence of legalized segregation as I had been accustomed to before joining the Army. At the time I was discharged from the Army, four years and one day from the day I enlisted, I had been greatly impacted by integration. I considered myself to be a convert to integration. My love for integration was equaled only by my hate for segregation. So great was my appreciation for integration that when I was discharged from the Army I decided not to return to my home in Alabama where my family, mother, sisters and brothers lived, but to go and live in Chicago. Eight days after I arrived in Chicago I got a job at the post

19

office. Now, with a job and enjoying the fruits of integration I was convinced that I had made the right decision to come to Chicago. There was not anything that I saw on the horizon to indicate that I would be leaving Chicago in the foreseeable future. All was well.

Ever since, even before I finished high school I wanted to go to college, but when I graduated from high school I did not have the necessary money to go to college. At that time, two of my sisters were in college and they were finding it difficult to stay in college despite the fact they were working on the campus a few hours every other day. While in the Army, from time-to-time, I thought about going to college when I returned to civilian life. I had enlisted in the Army because I was unable to go to college, and the main reason I did not re-enlist in the Army was because of my strong desire to go to college. First, I considered attending Roosevelt University and then several other institutions of higher learning in Chicago, but all of them were too expensive for me. I did not have sufficient finances to go to college in Chicago. It was rumored that a GI-Bill for the Korean War veterans would be enacted by the Congress, but no steps had been taken by any Congressperson to make it happen. Most people felt, just as I did, that no GI-Bill would be passed until the Korean War ended. I wanted to go to college the ensuing year that was less than a half year away. Two of my sisters had graduated from Alabama State College where the cost of attending college was less expensive than attending college in Chicago. But I did not want to return to the South. I remember asking myself: "Would I rather enjoy the fruits of integration in the North and not go to college or return to Alabama and go to college?" I received the answer: "Return to Alabama and go to college." When I told my pastor, Reverend Louis Rawls, pastor of the Greater Tabernacle Baptist Church, about my decision to return to Alabama and go to college, he said that I had made the right decision and predicted that I would be blessed and be a blessing to others in Alabama.

In early September, a few days before college began at Alabama State College, I decided to leave Chicago and return to Alabama and enroll at Alabama State College. Between summer and autumn in mid-September, I sat foot in Montgomery, one of the locations of the capitol of the Confederacy and the present capitol of Alabama. This was my first visit to Montgomery, the third largest city in Alabama. I had lived in Mobile, Alabama's second largest city for a half year before entering the military. I still had not visited Birmingham, that state's largest city. Immediately after arriving in Montgomery I enrolled in college. I was aware that most of my classmates were about four years younger than me. I was delightfully surprised when they elected me to be the president of the freshman class. From that very day I felt empowered and sensed, in a way, that I had the ability to be a leader. It was not that I had not assumed leadership roles in the past. Indeed, I had, including in the Army. But being elected by my classmates to be their leader gave me a different feeling than I had experienced before. One of the good things that happened to me as a result of being president of the freshman class was that I had the opportunity to develop a relationship with G. Garrick Hardy, dean of the Freshman College and a professor, who taught a freshman core humanities course. He was active in the community and headed the fund-raising drive for the March of Dimes in South Montgomery. Sometimes he selected me to accompany him to off-campus events and represent the freshman class or college. I still remember, as clearly as if it had happened yesterday, the parents-freshman class day held at Alabama State College. I was one of the speakers that day and I recall that I received the most enthusiastic applause rendered by the parents. Some of them personally congratulated me after the meeting. My experience as president of the freshman class was personally rewarding and, in a certain way, it launched my leadership career.

I first met Vernon Johns, pastor of the Dexter Avenue Baptist Church in November of 1952. He was a colorful personality who often challenged black people to improve their plight in life and begin doing that by ridding themselves of their fear of the white man. He advocated black self-help that included black people operating their own businesses. Johns was no ordinary preacher, although a pastor of the sophisticated members of Dexter Avenue Baptist Church who were mostly college professionals, he would roll-up his shirt sleeves and sometimes his pants, and sell watermelons, fish and other products on the streets from the back of his pickup truck, to the displeasure of some of his members. I attended the last of his three-lecture series on a Friday evening at the Dexter Avenue Baptist Church and heard him speak on "Religion." Without having once looked at a note he gave a hour and half lecture, quoting twelve scholars' definitions of religion before giving his own definition of religion. I was fascinated by what he had to say and the way he said it. One of the things he said during that lecture was "In Montgomery the only racial development that pierced through symbolism was President Harry S. Truman's executive order of July 26, 1948, ending segregation in the armed forces." Then he lampooned black people for their passivity and lack of involvement in achieving their own freedom. After many disagreements with some of the members of his congregation he offered his resignation, and in December he returned to Farmville, Virginia where he was born in 1892. His presence in Montgomery left a lasting impression on the people of that city. One year after he left Montgomery, the black people established, as he had urged them to do, a farmers market that was owned and operated by black people. I purchased five shares of stock in that enterprise.

In January 1953, General Dwight David Eisenhower was inaugurated as the thirty-fourth president of the United States. The black people in Montgomery, as was true of most black people, were not excited about him being president. They felt that he was a friend of and could become a tool for white Southerners. They were aware that white people in the South had voted in large numbers for him because they felt that he would support their efforts to maintain segregation and keep most black people disfranchised. It was common knowledge to black people that when President Truman decided to integrate the military, General Eisenhower urged him to keep the military segregated because, as he put it, "that would be better for both black and white soldiers." At the time Eisenhower was taking over the reign of the government, I was trying, without success, to become a registered voter in Alabama. Black people had wanted former Illinois Governor Adlai Stevenson to be the president. Black people had come to appreciate President Truman, to a degree. But they were highly skeptical of Eisenhower, notwithstanding his record as a military leader.

Upon the recommendation of Reverend H. H. Johnson, the

22

members of the Hall Street Baptist Church invited me to serve as their supply pastor, a term used for a minister serving as a pastor when a church does not have a pastor. They had terminated the employment of their former pastor because, in their words, "he had conducted himself in a fashion that was unbecoming of a pastor." I accepted the invitation to serve as their supply pastor while they conducted a search for a new pastor. This was a challenge for me, but I faced it with a measure of confidence, thanks to the Reverend Johnson who gave guidance and encouragement.

Upon learning that I was trying to become a registered voter, two professors at Alabama State College took a special interest in me. Jo Ann Robinson, president of the Women's Political Council and professor of English literature, and C. E. Pierce, a professor of economics. Subsequently, they both were my teachers. Professor Pierce said that he wanted me to meet E. D. Nixon who was the chief black leader in Montgomery. I could tell by his comments that he held Nixon in high esteem. As a matter of fact, he said that "Nixon is the only black man in Montgomery, now that Vernon Johns had left the city, who was doing anything positive to help black people achieve justice in Montgomery." Soon after my conversation with Pierce I met Nixon, a man who was over six feet tall with a commanding presence that exuded pride and self-confidence. He was a Pullman porter, member of the A. Philip Randolph's Brotherhood of Sleeping Car Porters, a past president of the Montgomery Branch of the NAACP and an outspoken advocate of justice for black people. He was the founder-president of the Progressive Democratic Association, a group composed of some of the black voters in Montgomery. It should be noted that Jo Ann Robinson's Women's Political Council was composed of some of Montgomery's black women voters. Both males and females were members of the Progressive Democratic Association, but their numbers were small. During my conversation with Nixon he encouraged me to continue to try to get registered to vote and offered to help me in any way that he could. He invited me to attend the next meetings of the Progressive Democratic Association.

It was necessary for me to make four appearances before the Voters Registration Board of Registrar of Voters, waiting, complaining and even threatening to take the Voters Registration Board to court, before I received my certificate of voters registration. After receiving my voters registration certificate I attended a meeting of the Progressive Democratic Association. Nixon and the other members of the Association were pleased that I had become a registered voter. Of course, no one seemed happier than Nixon, except me. He urged those present at the meeting to help get other people registered to vote. He said, "It ain't going to be easy to get people registered to vote but our people got to register to vote." Pointing to me he said, "Look what Fields has done." From that experience I learned that some things are worth fighting for and not to fight for them is to settle to be less than you were meant to be.

While serving during the interim period as the supply pastor at the Hall Street Baptist Church, I was called by the members of the Bell Street Baptist Church to be their pastor. Upon learning that I had been called to be the pastor of the Bell Street Baptist Church, the members of the Hall Street Baptist Church speeded up their selection process to select a pastor. I lost by only seven votes. Later the Chairman of the Deacons Board of the Hall Street Baptist Church told me that I was not selected to be their pastor because I was unmarried. "Some members of the church did not want a single man to be their pastor after what they had experienced with their recently terminated pastor," he told me, although the members had charged the former pastor with drinking rather than with sexual matters. Anyway, I had already accepted the invitation to be the pastor of the Bell Street Baptist Church before the vote was taken at the Hall Street Baptist Church. I was convinced that God wanted me to be the pastor of the Bell Street Baptist Church. On the first Sunday in July 1953, I preached my first sermon as the resident pastor of the Bell Street Baptist Church. My studies and pastoral duties kept me very busy. I was determined to do a good job both as a student and as a pastor. I did take time to work in Nixon's campaign. He was a candidate for committeeman, and as such he became the first black person to have his name appear on the ballot in Montgomery since the Reconstruction. He knew that he would not win without white support and he knew that white people would not vote for him. In running for the position he demonstrated that a black person could run for a political office in Montgomery, notwithstanding the fact that he received threats from white racists who warned him that he had better take his name off the ballot.

Today, May 17, 1954, the United States Supreme Court ruled in the "Brown v. Board of Education of Topeka" that "segregation is inherently unequal," and ordered a ban on segregation in public education. I was in the library when the librarian announced the Supreme Court's decision. Everyone I talked with were overjoyed. They all felt that the struggle to get black people into "white schools" would be difficult. Nixon expressed gratitude to the Supreme Court for making a just decision and predicted that the Ku Klux Klan whose members had burned crosses on his lawn on three different occasions during the last seven years would use violence to keep blacks away from white schools. I recalled that I was in the Army when president Truman issued his executive order banning segregation in the military. It was nearly two years later before I was placed in an integrated unit. I added that the important thing is that the Supreme Court's decision has put the law on the side of black people, something that oftentimes had not been true for black people. A case in point: the Supreme Court ruled in 1896 in "Plessy v. Ferguson," that segregation, including jimcroism, was constitutional. Court decisions such as that one, especially when they are rendered by the highest court in the land, reveal why people may choose to consider a revolution as being the only viable avenue available to them in their quest for justice. For more than a half century that Supreme Court's decision made it lawful for black people to be denied their citizenship rights. What a disgrace! But it is worth repeating: the May 17th decision by the Supreme Court was an honorable one that should benefit black people. Obviously, it was long overdue.

With the assistance of Jo Ann Robinson and a former president of the Women's Political Council, Mary Fair Burks, we established Club-21 on the Alabama State College campus. I was chosen to be president of the club. The objective of Club-21 was to assist students in preparing themselves to pass the written voters registration test. There was really no way to prepare them to pass the oral test, except to encourage them to persevere in their endeavor to become registered voters. Club-21 participants were also instructed as to how they could assist and encourage their parents to become registered voters. I was very pleased when a student we had drilled in the Alabama Constitution showed me his voters registration certificate that he had received the day before. The oral test, like poll tax that first-time voters except veterans had to pay, was a means used to keep blacks from qualifying to vote. Black college professors had failed the oral voter registration tests that were in some instances administered by elementary school drop-outs. Club-21 and the Women's Political Council were able to get the Montgomery County voters Registration Board to place a voting machine on the campus of Alabama State College that could be used by students who were interested in voting. During the year that I was elected president of the Student College Council, students used a voting machine to vote for Student College Council officers. This was the first time that this had ever been done at Alabama State College.

Occasionally I was guest preacher on Radio Station WRMA in Montgomery. That radio station was commonly referred to as the "black radio station," because the station's employees were black and it catered to black interests, particularly in matters of consumerism, more than other Montgomery radio stations. The radio station was owned by white folk. Oftentimes my sermons addressed social issues and were critical of segregation practices. One of my hard-hitting sermons on racism got me kicked off the air. I was cut off the air in the middle of my preaching. When I contacted the owner of the radio station about the matter I was told by him that in order for me to speak on that radio station I would have to preach on religion, not social matters. He also told me that he had received complaints from white folk about the kind of preaching I had done on the radio. Black people encouraged me and thanked me for having the courage to tell the truth about racism. Or, as one person said, "Telling it like it is."

Martin Luther King preached his first sermon as the resident pastor of the Dexter Avenue Baptist Church in early September 1954. A month later I met him on the campus of Alabama State College when he came to visit Juanita Brewer. She was a member of the Dexter Avenue Baptist Church and an employee at Alabama State College. Two days earlier she had invited me to come to her office at noon so that she could introduce me to her pastor. During my conversation with King I congratulated him on having been selected to be the pastor of Dexter Avenue Baptist Church and told him how glad I was to know that he had come to Montgomery. He congratulated me on being the pastor of the Bell Street Baptist Church and said that he had heard some good things about me. He also told me that he had completed his residential work at Boston University for the Ph.D. degree but still had to finish writing his dissertation. He added, "I am on my way to the library to do some research." The next day Mrs. Brewer wanted to know how did I find her new pastor?" I said, "He has real presence," and added, "Real presence is real love."

The students at Alabama State College elected me to be the president of the Student College Council during my senior year. My opponent for the office of president was T. Y. Rogers, a popular honor student. When the votes were counted I won nearly sixty percent of the votes and was elected the president. The student newspaper stated that I had been elected rather than Rogers because the students believed that I would fight for their interests and confront the president about improving the quality of life for students on the campus. They felt that Rogers would support the status quo and remain in the good graces of administrators. During our hotly contested campaign I stated that I would insist on students having better food in the cafeteria, that the curfew for female students be the same as that for male students and that the student fees be used to provide more social activities for the students, including more live entertainment. Rogers did not consider these issues. One of the crowning experiences I had during my reign as president of the Student College Council was crowning "Miss Alabama State" during the annual Thanksgiving Day football game between Alabama State College and Tuskegee Institute. The game was held in the Montgomery Coliseum, an arena where blacks were not permitted to frequent on any other occasion, with the exception of being employed as servants there. My leadership was felt on the campus that year. It was a year when there were student demonstrations on campus that included the burning down of some old unoccupied buildings on the campus. I recall the president's wife, Portia Trenholm, sent a message to me with the request that I come to her home which was located on the edge of the campus. During our conversation she pleaded with me to stop the student demonstrations.

Her husband, H. Council Trenholm, was being pressured by the white folk downtown who had ordered him to put an end to the student demonstrations. During our conversation she said, "Fields, you are the only person who can stop these demonstrations." I wanted to say to her, "I didn't start these demonstrations and I can't stop them," but instead I said, "I'll do what I can to help restore peace to the campus." I knew that the students were justified in complaining. They had long-standing grievances that the administration had refused to address.

In October 1954, I purchased a home in Mobile Height, a section of Montgomery where black middle-class people lived. Even though I had a thirty-year mortgage on it, I was proud to be a homeowner. My paternal grandfather, my hero if ever I had one, was a landowner. He taught me the importance of owning land, as did my father, who owned his own home. Had my father lived beyond my fourteenth birthday I believe that he would have been a sizable landowner the same as his father.

Claudette Colvin, a fifteen-year-old student at Booker T. Washington High School in Montgomery was arrested on March 2, 1955, for occupying a seat in the section of the bus designated for white bus riders. On May 6th Judge Eugene Carter found her guilty on an assault charge, and fined her ten dollars. She was a member of the Hutchinson Street Baptist Church where I was a member. Our pastor Rev. Johnson and I were present for her trial. Black people were hurt and displeased with Judge Carter's decision, but they had not expected him to rule differently. This case would not be sufficient to arouse black people enough to spur them into action, apart from expressing their thoughts about the injustice black people receive in the courts and elsewhere. One black leader, Reverend B. D. Lambert, endeavored to encourage black folk in Montgomery to do as the black people had done in Baton Rouge nearly two years earlier when they boycotted the buses beginning on June 23, 1953, under the leadership of Reverend Theodore J. Jemison. That boycott lasted for eight days. Apparently, the most positive result of that boycott was it kept some blacks' money out of whites' pockets.

In August 1955, I was awarded the B. S. degree in Teachers Education. After attending college for three consecutive years, including summers, I had succeeded in achieving a college degree. My experience as a student had empowered me with knowledge, helped me to become a better server of humankind and increased my joy. About a month after I graduated, in September 1955, I enrolled in the Masters of Education program at Alabama State College. Having about six months remaining on my GI-Bill was a factor that helped me to decide to continue my education without an interruption. I had entertained the thought of giving more time to the ministry for at least a year or two before going back to school. Now I had enrolled in Graduate School and was enjoying my studies more than ever. My ministry was also going great.

On October 15, 1955, Mary Louise Smith, a Montgomery resident, was arrested and fined for refusing to yield her seat to a white bus passenger. Black people were again concerned about her arrest as they had been earlier in the year with the arrest of Claudette Colvin, but no steps were taken by black people to become involved in pursuing justice in the case, except for Jo Ann Robinson's attempt to get black leaders involved in the case along with members of the Women Political Council. She was not successful. Nixon felt that because of the questionable character of Smith it would not be a good case to pursue. Robinson retorted, "Her shortcomings are irrelevant to the principles of the case." Nixon's decision prevailed and no further interest was expressed in this case. It did appear that some black people were more outraged about the mistreatment of black bus riders than they had been before.

December 1, 1955 through December 4, 1955 was the twilight period in Montgomery. Rosa Parks was arrested and jailed for refusing to give up her seat on the bus to a white man in violation of the segregation laws of Alabama. Black leaders issued their magna carta calling for a one-day boycott of buses. An article appeared in the *Montgomery Advertiser* announcing the pending boycott of buses by black people. Police Commissioner Clyde Sellers made pronouncements on television denouncing the boycott, and black pastors delivered from their pulpits admonishments directing black people not to ride the buses the next day.

Before the Montgomery Bus Boycott began in early December 1955, I was telling black people in Montgomery, sometimes preaching to them, three things that I was an example of: (1) become a registered voter, (2) get an education and (3) own your own home. Accomplishing this threesome was no small achievement for a twenty-five-year-old black man living in Alabama. I was acknowledged as a leader in Montgomery and respected by most black Montgomerians.

Little did I know at the time that something big was looming upon the horizon and hovering over the sometimes dreary skies of Montgomery that would soon put the city in the national spotlight. Get ready for a jolt with such enormous strength that it shook the walls of deep-South segregation with a force so powerful that their fall brought about the biggest change to take place in black-white relations in Montgomery since the end of the Reconstruction when black people were literally disfranchised and denied most citizenship rights that were freely enjoyed by white Americans.

When Vernon Johns returned to Montgomery to preach at the seventy-ninth anniversary of Dexter Avenue Baptist Church where he formerly pastored on December 9, 1956, just eight days before the United States Supreme Court rejected Alabama's final appeal and mandated desegregation on Montgomery buses, reflected upon a statement that he made four years earlier when he said that, "In Montgomery the only racial development that pierced through symbolism was President Truman's executive order of July 26, 1948, ending segregation in the armed forces," he exclaimed gleefully. "The Montgomery Bus Boycott is the breakthrough black people desperately needed and having already pierced through symbolism it will markedly change Montgomery and be the epiphany for liberation, justice and equality for black people throughout America."

PART TWO

The First Half of the Montgomery Bus Boycott

Rosa Parks was arrested and jailed for violating Alabama's segregation laws after she refused to give up her bus seat to a white man. This incident caused the black people in Montgomery to launch the Montgomery Bus Boycott four days later that was initially set to last for a day but continued for 382 days. On Thursday, December 1, 1955, about 4:30 in the afternoon, Parks left the Montgomery Fair department store where she was employed as a seamstress and boarded a bus for her Cleveland Avenue route at her usual bus stop on Court Square in downtown Montgomery that would take her to her home in West Montgomery. The thirty-six passenger bus was about two-thirds filled when it left Court Square. The passengers were seated in the traditional manner, as was practiced in Montgomery, blacks from rear toward front and whites from front toward rear. Usually about ten to fourteen seats, depending on the bus route, were reserved for white people. On this heavily traveled Cleveland Avenue route by blacks only twelve seats were reserved for whites. Sometimes seats reserved for whites would remain empty while blacks stood up. At other times blacks were required to leave their seats and give them to white passengers who boarded the bus after they were already seated, even if they had to stand up. The bus driver had full power to order a black person to move from his seat. Because of conditioning sometimes blacks would leave their seats without being asked to do so by the driver when they saw whites boarding the bus who would not have seats. Some blacks vacated their seats because they resented the white bus drivers saying anything to them, let alone telling them to move from their seats. One black bus rider expressed the feeling of rage he experienced when asked by a white bus driver to move out of his seat so a white person could have it this way: "It makes me feel like I would like to separate his head from the rest of his body." Blacks were all too aware that a bus driver, like a policeman, had the authority that was backed-up by a legalized segregation system to give them orders, including ordering them to get off the bus before they wanted to for no justifiable reason. In short, a bus driver had police power on the bus that he could use discriminatingly, in the worse sense of the meaning of the term, in dealing with black bus riders.

When the bus that Parks was on came to the second stop it picked up other passengers and when it reached the third stop, the thirty-six passenger bus was filled with twenty-six blacks and ten whites after a white person took the last empty seat. At that stop three white persons had boarded the bus who had no seats. The driver, J. D. Blake, asked four blacks, including Parks, to move out of their seats with the objective of providing seats for three white bus riders. The two black women sitting across the aisle from Parks moved from their seats as did the black man sitting next to her, but she remained in her seat that was next to the window. The driver noticed that a white man was standing up and that two white people were sitting parallel to Parks, which was also forbidden by the practice of segregation laws. He came near Parks and asked her to move. Parks refused to move. He said to her, "Look woman, I told you to move. You better make it easy on yourself and move out that seat. Are you going to stand up?" Parks replied, "No, I am not in the white section of the bus." Blake reminded her that the white section was where he said it was and that he had told her that she was in it. Then he added, "That's the law!" as to say in the same breath, "I am the law!" Further insistence of a threatening nature by the driver that she move did not cause Parks to leave her seat. Blake then notified her that she was under arrest and that she would not move until he returned with regular Montgomery police. Parks remained in her seat seemingly unperturbed. Blake phoned the police and within minutes F. B. Day and D. W. Nixon entered that bus. Policeman Day asked Parks "Why didn't you stand up when the driver asked you to?" Parks replied, "I didn't think that there was any reason that I should have to." She was arrested, taken to the police station where she was booked, fingerprinted, photographed and incarcerated.

Parks called her mother, who panicked upon hearing that her

daughter had been arrested and was in jail. In the meantime a passenger on the bus told a friend of Parks about the event, and that friend, Bertha Butler, immediately called the home of E. D. Nixon, Montgomery's chief black leader. Parks' mother also called Nixon about the same time. Nixon was not at home, but his wife, Arlet, was, and she phoned her husband's small downtown office. Nixon was out of his office when she called, but when he returned he got the message and called his wife. "What's up?" he asked his wife. She told him that Rosa Parks had been arrested and taken to jail, but she didn't know what for. Then she said to him, "Go get her out of jail." Nixon immediately called the police station and inquired as to what Parks had been arrested for. The desk officer rudely told him that the charges against her were none of his business. Nixon called Fred Gray's office, but Gray was out of the city. He then called Charles Langford, the only other black attorney in Montgomery, but was unable to reach him. Nixon called a white lawyer, Clifford Durr, a liberal, with whom he had become friendly with since having met him and his wife some years earlier when Durr served with the Federal Communications Commission before he and his wife Virginia returned to their native Alabama. Nixon told Durr what he knew about Park's arrest. Durr promised to find out what he could from the jail and call him back as soon as he heard anything. When he called back he told Nixon that Parks was charged with violating the segregation laws of Alabama. That was it. Nixon told him that he was going and pay the $100 bond to secure Parks' release. Durr asked him to come by his home and pick him up. When Nixon arrived at the Durr's home, Virginia was also waiting with her husband and ready to make the trip to the jail. On their way to the jail they discussed the possibility of Parks being a test case in the courts. Once at the jail the desk officer instinctively handed the bond papers to Clifford Durr, even though Nixon was standing closer to him, for signature. Durr told him, no, Nixon, a property owner, would be the man to sign. Nixon owned a home located at 647 Clinton Street in Montgomery, which in 1986 was added to the Alabama Register of Landmarks and Heritage by the Alabama Historical Commission. Parks was released and they brought her home. While the Durrs waited in the car, Nixon escorted Parks into her home. He asked her mother and husband to please be excused for a brief while so he could speak to Parks alone. Nixon asked her one question, would she be willing to fight the case in court? He told her he felt that this is the right case and that she is the right person to be involved in a test case that could end up going all the way to the Supreme Court before it was over. Parks was not convinced immediately that she was the right person, but after listening more to the persuasive Nixon who she highly respected, said, "If you think it is all right, I'll go with you." She knew that her husband was extremely fearful of white reprisals and that her mother was not enthusiastic about her becoming involved in a court case, not realizing that she had a trial coming up on Monday. But they all had one thing in common, they trusted Nixon.

Meanwhile, Fred Gray had received the message about the arrest. After talking with Parks and agreeing to represent her, he called Jo Ann Robinson, the president of the Women's Political Council. This organization throughout the early 1950s had been active in providing leadership for the black community, sometimes in conjunction with Nixon or as a rival of him for active leadership in the black community. The group had also joined with the Citizens Steering Committee, headed by Rufus Lewis, a businessman and proprietor of a classic night club. There was evidence that these two groups, that is, their leaders and some of their members, felt that they had an advantage over Nixon because they were college graduates. Nixon had only a few years of formal education. Yet, they realized that Nixon was a Pullman porter whose job took him to Chicago and northern cities and that he had been a member of A. Philip Randolph's Brotherhood of Sleeping Car Porters. Beyond that they realized that Nixon was a highly respected leader in the black community. Robinson, Lewis and Nixon knew that they needed each other and that the black community needed their leadership. They made up the only non-ministerial black leadership in Montgomery.

After learning of the arrest of Parks that Thursday night, Robinson called some of her colleagues who were members of the Women's Political Council, and told them to meet her at Alabama State College. She impressed upon them that this was a SOS, and that she had spoken to Nixon and Gray about Parks' arrest. She told her colleagues that she needed them to come and help her take care of some urgent business. These women came and they worked into the

34

wee hours of the morning. They agreed on the statement that follows which they mimeographed at Alabama State College:

Another Negro woman has been arrested and thrown into jail because she refused to get up out of her seat on the bus for a white person to sit down.

It is the second time since the Claudette Colbert (sis) case that a Negro woman has been arrested for the same thing. This has to be stopped. Negroes have rights, too, for if Negroes did not ride the buses, they could not operate. Three-forth of the riders are Negroes, yet we are arrested, or have to stand over empty seats. If we do not do something to stop these arrests, they will continue. The next time it may be you, or your daughter, or mother.

This woman's case will come up on Monday. We are, therefore, asking every Negro to stay off the buses Monday in protest of the arrest and trial. Don't ride the buses to work, to town, to school, or anywhere on Monday.

You can also afford to stay out of town for one day. If you work take a cab or walk. But please, children and grown-ups, don't ride the bus at all on Monday. Please stay off all buses Monday.

The next morning about 4:30 a.m., Robinson called Nixon in the hopes that she would reach him before he left the city for his Pullman train trip. She explained to him what the women of the Women's Political Council who had met with her had done and their suggestion that blacks boycott the buses on Monday. Nixon immediately gave his approval to the proposal to boycott the buses and said that he would begin calling ministers and ask them to meet with her and other members of their group at the Dexter Avenue Baptist Church on Friday evening so they can endorse and declare their support for the plan. Robinson told him that she would have a courier to bring him a few copies of the leaflet announcing the boycott within fifteen minutes. Nixon had always respected and received respect from ministers. He began calling ministers. His first call was made to Ralph D. Abernathy, pastor of the First Baptist Church. Abernathy agreed to support the effort. Then he called his pastor, H. H. Hubbard, pastor of the Bethel Baptist Church. Next he called Martin Luther King, Jr., pastor of the Dexter Avenue Baptist

Church. Then he called A. W. Wilson, pastor of the Holt Street Baptist Church. I learned nearly twenty-two years later when Nixon visited Los Angeles where I was living at the time in October 1977, when he told the Los Angeles Interdenominational Ministerial Alliance that was honoring him with an "Award for Outstanding Service," that I, Uriah J. Fields, pastor of the Bell Street Baptist Church, was the fifth person that he called. He also called some other ministers.

Nixon called Joe Azbell, editor of the *Montgomery Advertiser*, and asked him to meet him at the train station to receive some important information that he wanted to share with him. Before boarding this Pullman run train, bound for Atlanta and on to Chicago and back, Nixon informed Azbell of blacks' plan to boycott the Montgomery buses on Monday. He gave him a copy of the leaflet announcing the boycott and asked him to carry the story about the bus boycott in the "Advertiser." Azbell told him that he would and that it will be the hottest story about a Montgomery event to appear in the "Advertiser" in many years. Nixon had disregarded the thinking of other black leaders who had wanted to keep the boycott a secret, i.e., a secret from white folk. Later Nixon explained why he decided to release the boycott plan to the "Advertiser," which proved to be a good thing.

That Friday evening about thirty-five black leaders met in the basement of the Dexter Avenue Baptist Church to discuss the impending boycott of buses on Monday and the Parks' trial that was also to be held on Monday. After a heated discussion that involved three leaders, including Rev. L. Roy Bennett, President of the Interdenominational Ministerial Alliance, who opposed a one-day boycott of the buses, the majority of those present voted in favor of staging a one-day bus boycott. It was also agreed upon that the statement Robinson and the women had produced be revised and that a mass meeting be held on Monday at 7:00 p.m., at the Holt Street Baptist Church. Below is the revised statement that was mimeographed and circulated in the black community:

Don't ride the bus to work, to town, to school, or any other place Monday, December 5
Another Negro Woman has been arrested and put in jail because

she refused to give up her bus seat.
Don't ride the buses to work, to town, to school or any where on
Monday. If you work take a cab, or share a ride , or walk.
Come to a mass meeting, Monday at 7:00 p.m., at the Holt Street
Baptist Church for further instruction.

Before the meeting adjourned all persons present were urged by
Robinson and some other leaders to distribute the leaflets that would
be ready mid-morning Saturday. All were urged to be present at the
Court House on Monday at 9:00 a.m., for Parks' trial. Ministers and
other leaders agreed to meet at Rev. Bennett's Mt. Zion AMEZ
Church at 2:00 p.m., Monday, to consider what response blacks
should make with regards to the decision that the judge will be
rendering in the Parks' trial and to prepare the program for the
Monday evening's mass meeting. A final plea was addressed to
pastors, urging them to announce from their pulpits Sunday that
blacks are to stay off the buses on Monday.

Early Saturday morning some leaflets were distributed in the
black community calling for a boycott of buses on Monday. That
evening a bus driver brought the bus line company manager, James
H. Bagley, a copy of the leaflet that he had found in his bus that
called for a boycott of buses on Monday.

The Saturday evening, *Alabama Journal* carried a brief statement
written by Joe Azbell stating that blacks plan to boycott the buses on
Monday. But it was Azbell's longer story headlined "Negro Groups
Ready Bus Boycott of Bus Lines" that appeared in the Sunday
Montgomery "Advertiser" that got the attention of a significant
number of Montgomerians, including other news media people. The
newspaper story also reported that Montgomery had been flooded
with thousands of copies of the leaflets announcing the boycott and
pointed out that Rev. A.W. Wilson said that the mass meeting would
be open to people of all races.

Nixon returned from his train run to discover that Joe Azbell had
written the article he had promised to write announcing blacks' plan
to stage a one-day bus boycott on tomorrow. He had felt, perhaps
before any other black leader, that getting this story in the newspaper
was the thing to do because it would inform some black people about
the proposed boycott who would not hear about it from any other

source. He felt that white people knowing about the proposed boycott would not in any way have an adverse effect on the anticipated boycott of buses.

The first Sunday of the month is the day when Holy Communion is administered in most black churches in Montgomery and the Sunday when more people attend church than any other Sunday of the month, except Easter Sunday. This was also the Sunday before the bus boycott would begin and the day before Parks' trial. That Sunday some ministers focused their sermons on the trial of Parks and the proposed boycott. I often preached sermons on social issues. After I had explained to my congregation the importance of taking a stand against evil and emphasizing that segregation was the evil that accounted for the arrest of Parks and her pending trial, I urged my parishioners to stay off buses on Monday, attend the Parks' trial at 9:00 a.m., on Monday, if possible, and, by all means, to meet at the Holt Street Baptist Church on Monday evening at 7:00 p.m., to receive some important information. Then I announced my subject: "The Trial of Jesus." During that sermon I dramatized how evil and sin accounted for both Jesus' and Parks' trials. I also demonstrated how the trial of Jesus had prepared us for Parks' trial. Following my sermon Holy Communion was administered. I had not remembered the congregation singing "Must Jesus Bear the Cross Alone," with so much passion and fervor as they did that Sunday. I got a feeling that everyone present felt that he or she had a part to play in suffering for righteousness' sake as we sang:

Must Jesus bear the cross alone,
And all the world go free?
No, there's a cross for everyone,
And there's a cross for me.

Later in the day I learned that some other ministers had taken a similar approach as I had during their Sunday services in their endeavor to persuade their members to support the boycott. Soon after I returned home and turned on my radio I heard a news reporter say, "Negroes are planning to boycott city buses tomorrow." Later that evening Police Commissioner Clyde Sellers, a rabid racist, appeared on local television to criticize black leaders for calling a bus boycott which he said cannot work. He also said that Montgomery policemen would stand ready tomorrow to assist those black citizens who wanted to ride the buses and he promised to deal appropriately with black "goon squads," who he claimed had been organized to intimidate blacks who otherwise would keep on riding the buses. Sellers' television appearance also informed blacks who had not been reached by the door-to-door campaign, the Sunday morning *Montgomery Advertiser*, and those who had not attended church that blacks would be boycotting buses on tomorrow. By Sunday evening, the night before the boycott, black leaders other than Nixon were expressing their satisfaction for the publicity that had been given to the proposed boycott, including that from Sellers.

Early Monday morning, December 5, 1955, just as dawn was on the horizon, I rose from my bed and turned on the radio to listen to the news. I heard a news reporter say, "People are waiting to see if Negroes will stay off the buses today. Bus Company Manager Bagley said that buses will run just as they normally do on all bus lines and that he expected everything to be normal." After eating breakfast, I left my home in Mobile Heights and headed east on Mobile Road until I reached Oak Street where I turned left. At the intersection of Oak Street and Day Street I saw a bus with only one passenger. I could not tell his race. However, that indicated to me that people were, indeed, staying off the buses today. Then I realized that it was much too early in the day for me to come to any conclusion regarding the success of the bus boycott or if there would be one. I drove a short distance to the Bell Street Baptist Church which is also located on Oak Street and picked-up a notebook. Minutes after leaving the church I saw a woman and a man walking. I stopped and asked them if they wanted a ride. They gladly accepted my offer. The man said that they usually ride the bus, but decided that they would not ride it today. I commended them for their decision not to ride the bus today. I told them that I was on my way to Park's trial. The woman expressed satisfaction with seeing black leaders stand up for their people and added, "This is something that we have needed for a long time."

When I arrived at the courthouse about 8:30 a.m., where Parks' trial would be held, the court room was nearly filled. At 9:00 a.m., Parks' trial got underway before City Court Judge John B. Scott.

Prosecutor Eugene Lowe dropped the charge of Parks' violation of Montgomery's segregation ordinance and substituted in its place one based upon a 1945 state law. That law mandated segregation and awarded drivers unlimited power to enforce it. Bus driver Blake was placed on the stand and asked to describe the incident, followed by two white women riders who supported the driver's account of what happened. Defense Attorney Gray challenged the validity of the segregation laws, but Judge Scott immediately announced his verdict guilty, with a $10.00 fine. Gray stated that he would appeal. The entire proceeding took seven minutes. Nixon walked out of the courtroom to post bond for her release.

Including those who had witnessed the trial, there were about four hundred people at the courthouse and none of them had taken a bus to get there. Two things were mentioned in the conversations that I heard immediately following Parks' conviction: "will the case be appealed?" and "I'll see you at the mass meeting at 7:00 p.m." Some leaders were also saying to each other, as I said to several persons, "I'll see you at the meeting at Mt. Zion AMEZ Church at 2:00 p.m." Before going home I drove down South Jackson Street to Alabama State College where I was a student. It seemed that most of the students and teachers had already heard that Parks had been found guilty and fined. I talked with several teachers, including Pierce and Brewer. They both agreed that appealing the case was the right thing to do. They encouraged me to stand up for them and expressed their concern that some black leaders may not be inclined to continue the fight, based on their past experiences with some of them. I got the impression that they would be attending the mass meeting later that evening. After I picked up a class assignment from a classmate for a class I had missed, I headed to a nearby restaurant and ate a light lunch. While driving toward the Mt. Zion AMEZ Church I saw two buses that were empty except for the drivers. Then I saw a bus that had five blacks on it and another one that had three blacks and six whites. Reflecting on the latter I asked myself, "When had I last saw a bus in this area with more whites than blacks? I still was not convinced that the not-as-yet one-day old bus boycott would be a success. However, I reasoned that if people didn't take the bus going they probably wouldn't take it returning to their homes.

About 1:45 p.m., I arrived at the Mt. Zion AMEZ Church. Nixon and some of the other people who would attend the meeting were already there. King was one of the last persons to arrive. When he arrived, he started to offer an apology for being late. Nixon interrupted him and said, "We'll forgive you Rev. King; you have a new baby." Everyone began laughing. Yolanda, Rev. King's and his wife's first child, was only three weeks old. But the laughter was short-lived. Everyone here knew that this would be a serious meeting because we faced a heavy challenge that was only equaled by the responsibility we felt that was ours to assume. The meeting had been called under the auspices of the Interdenominational Ministerial Alliance of which Rev. L. Roy Bennett was the President, rather than under the auspices of the Baptist Ministers' Conference of which Rev. H. H. Hubbard was president. Abernathy, secretary of the Baptist Ministers' Conference, had tried unsuccessfully to have the meeting at the Baptist Center where Rev. H. H. Hubbard would have likely been the presiding officer. But most people who participated in making the decision about the meeting felt that if the meeting was under the auspices of the Baptist people, ministers from other denominations would be less likely to be supportive. The Baptist denomination was larger than all the other denominations combined among blacks and some people belonging to other denominations had expressed on more than a few occasions that they felt that Baptists wanted to dominate everything. So Bennett, a Methodist, also the pastor of the Mt. Zion AMEZ Church where the meeting was being held, had been chosen to be the presiding officer at this meeting.

The time had come for the meeting to begin. Bennett called the meeting to order. He was presiding by virtue of his office as president of the IMA and not because the leaders assembled had any particular confidence in his leadership. It was clear to me that some people present had accepted Bennet's leadership only in the name of unity. It was a defaulting situation that had elevated Bennett to the presidency of the IMA. After prayer was offered by Hubbard, Bennett immediately turned to Nixon and asked him to discuss the purpose of the meeting. Nixon was blunt and to the point. He said that we must seize this opportunity to do something about the mistreatment Negroes have been experiencing on buses. He commented on the Parks' conviction and asserted that what happened today in the courtroom was not the end of this case. Then he challenged Negroes to stand up this one time for what was right. Abernathy was the next person to speak. He mentioned the success of today's boycott. Then he asked whether or not we are going to have a new organization or whether one of the existing organizations would be the channel through which we would operate. Some participants felt that the Interdenominational Ministerial Alliance would be the proper channel through which we would operate. They emphasized that the non-political and interdenominational character of the IMA makes it the most suitable organization for dealing with the mistreatment of blacks on buses. Reflecting on a Social Psychology college course I was currently taking which focused on small groups and a discussion we recently had on the "leaderless group" I said, facetiously, "Maybe we can have a leaderless group." Then seriously I said, "Since the leadership for the task we are committing ourselves to is not just for ministers, and I called the names of several persons present who were not ministers, I think that we should have an organization that is not religious, that is, one that does not have a religious name at a minimum." Rufus Lewis, Abernathy, Bennett and Johnson agreed with the point I had made. By consensus It was decided that we form a new organization. Bennett wanted to know what name are we going to give to the organization? Abernathy said, "I know, Brother Nixon, you are the president of the Progressive Democratic Association. I would like to suggest that we name our new organization the Montgomery Improvement Association." Then he added, "rather than the IMA we will be the MIA." Abernathy's suggestion lightened up things enough for people to laugh again just as they had done when Nixon commented on King's new baby accounting for him being late for the meeting. After no one else suggested another name Abernathy made a motion that the name of the organization be the Montgomery Improvement Association. The motion was seconded by J. W. Bonner, pastor of the first CME Church and approved. Bennett then asked, "Who shall be the officers?" Edgar Nathaniel French, pastor of the Hillard Chapel AME Zion Church wanted to know what officers do we need. It was agreed that we should elect a president, vice-president, recording secretary, corresponding secretary, financial secretary and treasurer. French said, "So we need six officers." That would be one-third of those present for this meeting. Bennett seemed to have had a premonition, rightly or wrongly, that he might be elected president, perhaps because he was presiding or maybe because someone had expressed the idea that the IMA would be the appropriate organization through which we could address the problem of the mistreatment of blacks on buses. Being the leader of this new organization was something that Bennett definitely did not want, mainly because he, like most people in that room, had fear in their hearts. They feared what white racists might do to them. So despite the fact that Bennett's ego was sometimes on the front burner, so to speak, he did not want to be president of the newly formed organization. It was fear that had kept nearly one-half of the thirty-five people who had met at the Dexter Avenue Baptist Church on Friday from attending this meeting. Before anyone else could nominate a person to be president, Bennett said, "I want to make a motion, but I will need somebody else to preside while I make it." After suggesting that Hubbard preside while he make his motion and temporarily relinquishing his post, he nominated M. L. King, Jr., to be president. His motion seconded by Rufus Lewis was approved. Hubbard had got his chance to preside briefly before returning the gavel to Bennett. Abernathy said, "King is a good man." To that Nixon gave a "ditto." King did not show any sign of being eager to serve in that position. A number of people did not want to be president and some who voted for King to be president did not feel that they were doing him a favor. Bennett resumed presiding. French nominated Bennett to be the vice-president. The motion was seconded by P. E. Conley, an evangelist, and approved. Bennett had been involved with organizations enough to know that being vice-president was not the same as being president, especially as far as responsibilities are concerned. Hubbard made a motion that Uriah J. Fields be the recording secretary. Erna A. Dungee seconded that motion, which was approved. Abernathy nominated Edgar N. French to be the corresponding secretary. That motion seconded by W. F. Alford, pastor of Beulah Baptist Church, was approved. Jo Ann Robinson nominated Erna A. Dungee to be the financial secretary. That motion was seconded by Lewis and approved. Hubbard prefaced his nomination saying, "There is not but one person here who qualifies to be the treasurer. He got money and he knows how to handle it." Nixon purportedly was the highest contributing member in Hubbard's Church. Hubbard nominated Nixon to be treasurer. King seconded that motion, which was approved.

It was suggested by H. H. Johnson, pastor of the Hutchinson Street Baptist Church, that we form an Executive Board. After some discussion it was agreed upon that the Executive Board be composed of twenty-five members who would represent a broad spectrum of community leadership. A motion to that effect was made by Johnson and seconded by James Roseby Glasco, director of the Negro Baptist Center. It was approved. Another motion was made by this writer and seconded by Robert L. Matthews, president of the local branch of the NAACP, that all persons present at this meeting be members of the Executive Board and that seven other persons be added at a later date. The motion was approved.

Bennett presented King, the newly elected president, and asked him to preside over the remainder of the meeting. King appeared to be a bit reluctant to preside during the remainder of the meeting and suggested that Bennett, who had done a good job, might continue to preside. However, recognizing that seemingly everyone in that room wanted him to preside, he expressed thanks to everyone for the confidence that he or she had placed in him. He said, "You have much more to offer than I do. I am sure that people like Nixon, Lewis and Abernathy could do a better job than I can. I promise to do my best." Then he commented on Parks' conviction and the success of today's boycott. At that point several other persons reported on what they had observed and expressed the belief that they felt that the boycott was a success. King said the question that we still must consider before this meeting adjourns is: "Where do we go from here?" He asked another question before anyone could respond to that question: "What are we going to say to the people who will be at the mass meeting this evening?" The consensus was that we appoint a committee to draw up a resolution that expresses our intention. Most of those present felt that the resolution should contain the issues that we are concerned about and the demands we are making on the city officials and Montgomery City Lines officials. In addition, the resolution should let the people know what they will be required to do to support any plan that is to be undertaken. King asked Abernathy to serve as the chairman of the Resolutions

Committee and suggested that he name other members of the committee. Abernathy selected Fred Gray, French, Nixon, (but Nixon, who was not known to work under other local leaders, declined) and Willie Frank Alford. The members of the Resolutions Committee were asked by Abernathy to remain after the meeting adjourns.

Additional discussion made it clear that most of those present wanted the bus boycott to continue. However, there were two or three older ministers who were not enthusiastic about continuing the boycott beyond one day. Two of them suggested that we discontinue the boycott because without it we could be more effective in negotiating with the city and bus line officials. No final decision was made at that meeting as to whether we would continue the boycott, i.e., no vote was taken on that matter, but it was obvious to me that the key persons, including King, Abernathy, Nixon, Robinson, Lewis, Johnson, French, Matthews, Dungee, Hubbard, and myself, were definitely for continuing the boycott. We all agreed that we should let the people attending the mass meeting decide as to whether or not the boycott would continue. Erna Dungee, a former school teacher, made the last remark on that matter when she said, "If black folk in Baton Rouge could boycott buses for over a week surely we can do the same thing in Montgomery." Bennett announced that Rev. Wilson told him that the press would be present for the mass meeting.

Attention shifted to the evening program, particularly regarding the persons who would speak at the mass meeting. Nixon, upon noticing that ministers were slow to make themselves available to be on the program, perhaps, because the news media was going to be at the meeting said, "Somebody in this thing has to get faith. I am just ashamed of you. You said that God has called you to lead the people and now you are afraid because your picture might get in the newspaper or on TV. Somebody has got to get hurt in this thing and if you preachers are not the leaders, then we need to pray that God will send us some other leaders." Every minister present denied in a chorus-like fashion that he was not afraid. But Nixon had spoken a truth that pierced the hearts of probably every person present. Some people feared not just for themselves, but for their families and their parishioners. They were aware that even their church buildings might become the targets for racists' abuse. Without anyone volunteering the following program was planned:

1. Opening Hymn - "Onward Christian Soldier"
2. Prayer - Rev. Willie Frank Alford
3. Scripture - Rev. U. J. Fields
4. Occasion - Rev. M. L. King, Jr.
   Presentation of Mrs. Rosa Parks - Rev. E. N. French
   Acknowledgment of Fred Daniel
5. Resolutions - Rev. Ralph D. Abemathy
   Vote on Recommendations
6. Offering - Rev. J. W. Bonner
7. Closing Hymn - "My Country 'Tis of Thee"
8. Benediction - Rev. L. Roy Bennett

With the completion of the program the meeting stood adjourned. Abernathy and other members of the Resolutions Committee and King remained to work on the resolution and recommendations that would be submitted to the people attending the mass meeting later that evening.

The names of the eighteen persons who participated in the meeting that was held for the purpose of organizing the Montgomery Improvement Association and electing the officers for that organization and planning the program for the first bus boycott mass meeting are as follows:

Ralph David Abernathy, Pastor of the First Baptist Church

L. Roy Bennett, Pastor of the Mt. Zion African Methodist Episcopal Church

J. W. Bonner, Pastor of the First Colored Methodist Episcopal Church

P. E. Conley, Evangelist and Businessman

Erna A. Dungee, Former school teacher and a founder of the Women's Political Council

Uriah J. Fields, Pastor of the Bell Street Baptist Church

Edgar Nathaniel French, Pastor of the Hillard Chapel African Methodist Episcopal Zion Church

Roseby James Glasco, Sr., Director of the Alabama Negro Baptist

Center (Montgomery)

Hillman H. Hubbard, Pastor of the Bethel Baptist Church

Henry H. Johnson, Pastor of the Hutchinson Street Baptist Church

Martin Luther King, Jr., Pastor of the Dexter Avenue Baptist Church

Rufus Andrews Lewis, Proprietor of the Citizens Club (a social club)

Robert L. Matthews, President of the Montgomery Branch of the NAACP and an Insurance company executive

Edgar Daniel Nixon, President of the Progressive Democratic Association and Human Rights leader

William J. Powell, Pastor of Old Ship African Methodist Episcopal Zion Church

Jo. Ann Robinson, Professor of English Literature at Alabama State College and President of the Women's Political Council

Arthur W. Wilson, Pastor of the Holt Street Baptist Church.

I could say that I regret having to disappoint some people who find much satisfaction in inflating and exaggerating numbers and other facts, as so many people have done who have written about the Montgomery Bus Boycott, but I have no such regret. Some people would increase the number of people who were present for the meeting held on December 5, 1955 when the Montgomery Improvement Association was founded and Martin Luther King, Jr. was elected its president. Thanks to Stanford University historian Clayborne Carson, Senior editor of "The Papers of Martin Luther King, Jr. (Vol. III)," who sent me a copy of the minute that I recorded on that day in my own handwriting that stated that eighteen persons were present on December 5, 1955 at the founding meeting of the Montgomery Improvement Association. The minute may also suggest that I know as much as anyone about what happened at that meeting. And, as the reader has already noticed that I read the scripture at the first mass meeting. Of course, I did promise that I would give an insider's testimony of the Montgomery Bus Boycott and tell the truth.

The first mass meeting of the Montgomery But Boycott was held Monday evening, December 5, 1955 at the Holt Street Baptist Church. When I arrived fifteen minutes before the 7:00 p.m. meeting was scheduled to begin the church auditorium was filled and people had congregated outside of the church in a huge mass. I made my way to Dr. Wilson's office where some other ministers and leaders had already gathered. Soon Wilson told the anxious crowd that exuded high expectancy accompanied by suspense that the meeting would begin within a few minutes. The people joined in singing "Onward Christian Soldier," reverently and with gusto. The first stanza of that song and refrain seemed to have conveyed the mood of those present:

> *Onward Christian soldiers! Marching as to war,*
> *With the cross of Jesus Going on before.*
> *Christ, the royal Master, Leads against the foe;*
> *Forward into battle, See his banner go.*
> *Refrain: Onward, Christian Soldiers, Marching as to war,*
> *With the cross of Jesus Going on before.*

After singing that song, including two other stanzas, the people joined in singing "Leaning on the Everlasting Arms." This song speaks of fellowship, walking, peace, and the security that is found in "leaning on the everlasting arms" of Jesus. There is a phrase in the song that says "O how sweet to walk..." This would become the daily mantra for boycotters during the next three hundred and eighty-one days as they walked in the spirit of Mother Pollard who might have been present for that first mass meeting. From time to time King quoted her as having said, "My feets is tired, but my soul is rested."

Without being introduced, Rev. Willie Frank Alford offered prayer. In his prayer he asked for increased faith to match the challenges that lie ahead, for love, understanding and for protection. He ended his prayer with this paraphrasing of Josiah Gilbert Holland's poem:

> *God give us leaders!*
> *A time like this demands;*
> *Strong minds, loving hearts,*
> *true faith, and feet to walk*
> *and follow you.*

Give us leaders that will
lead where you direct.

Following that moving prayer I read from the Thirty-fourth Psalm
that I selected because I felt that we should begin with putting God
first. That Psalm opened with these words:

I will bless the Lord at all times;
His praise shall continually be in my mouth."

I deliberately repeated and with emphasis the nineteenth verse
which says:

Many are the afflictions of the righteous,
but the Lord delivereth him out of them all."

Reverend Wilson escorted Rev. King to the lectern and simply
said: "Rev. King will give the occasion." King thanked Wilson, and
seemingly in the same breath mentioned how happy he was to see
each person. Then he stated that we were here on serious business.
Continuing, he recounted some of the injustices black people have
been subjected to in America and, more specifically, in Montgomery,
as he underscored how democracy had failed black people. Then he
turned his attention to Rosa Parks, her arrest last Thursday and her
trial that had been held earlier that day. King said there is some
unresolved business that has brought us here on this occasion. "Mrs.
Parks is a fine woman," he wanted the people to know. The people
gave a verbal response of agreement and a loud applause. Reverend
Edgar Nathaniel French came forth and presented Mrs. Parks. She
received a thunderous applause. French said that he would like to
present a young man: "This is Fred Daniel, a student at Alabama
State College and a member of the First Baptist Church." Continuing
he said, "Early this morning this young man was arrested on a
disorderly conduct charge (later it was dismissed) for allegedly
preventing a woman from getting on a bus." Daniel received a hearty
applause from the people.

King continued to laud and pay tribute to Parks and promised
Daniel our support. He predicted that there would be many others

who would be subjected to police abuse and added that these things won't stop us from doing what we must do if we are going to receive justice. He called upon everyone to unite, to join hands and hearts together, and go out from this place resolved not to retreat one inch until we have been accorded full respect and granted our rights. At the end of his statement the people gave him a thunderous applause. Next , he introduced Reverend Abernathy and stated that he would come to us and read the resolution and recommendations. The people were admonished by King to listen carefully and with interest so they would know everything that was said, because they would be asked to vote on these recommendations.

Abernathy thanked King and said, "All of you who know me, know very well that I would love to make a speech now." The people exploded with laughter because many of them knew that Abernathy was telling the truth. He had a knack for wanting to improve on what someone else had said or by making some addition to what someone else had said, perhaps, to draw some attention to himself. After talking about justice, freedom and equality of opportunity, equality of participation and equality of achievement, he began reading the resolutions that had been drawn up by the Resolutions Committee he chaired. After about ten or eleven "Whereases" that recounted a series of injustices that black people had experienced in Montgomery, some of them involving mistreatment of black bus riders, he said, "In light of these observations, be it therefore resolved: 'Number one: That the citizens of Montgomery are requesting that every citizen in Montgomery, regardless of race, color, or creed, refrain from riding buses owned and operated in the City of Montgomery by the Montgomery City Lines, Incorporated, until some arrangement has been worked out between said citizens and the Montgomery City Lines, Incorporated.'" He also read a number two and number three that called upon people with automobiles to assist those in need of transportation and for employers to provide transportation for their own employees. The recommendations were : "(1) that more courteous treatment of Negro passengers by bus operators be guaranteed, (2) that seating be on a first-come, first served basis, with Negroes continuing to sit from the rear of the bus and white from front to rear and that no seat would be designated as solely for white or Negro passengers, (3) that Negro operators be employed on predominately Negro routes." The understanding, as reflected in these recommendations, was that blacks would continue to boycott buses until these demands were granted by the City of Montgomery and the Montgomery City Lines officials. Finally, Abernathy said that we had no intention of using any unlawful means or any intimidation to persuade persons not to ride the Montgomery City Lines buses. Each person's own conscience should be his guide, he said. The people had applauded a number of times while Abernathy read the resolution and recommendations, but at the end of his reading there was extended applause and "all rights," "yeses" and "that's its," exclaimed. Abernathy offered a motion, stating: "I move that this resolution and these recommendations shall be adopted."

King joined with a number of people in seconding the motion that was seconded by many people rather than by any particular person. However, I wrote in my minute that the motion was seconded by Nixon. I did that because no single person had done more to bring black people in Montgomery to the place where they were standing than Nixon. King then said, "It has been moved and seconded that this resolution and these recommendations would be accepted and adopted by the citizens of Montgomery. Are you ready for the question?" "Yes" was proclaimed with an earthquake-like shout. When he asked for opposers to vote, there was only laughter that conveyed a dare anyone to opposed or a recognition that there was nobody who wanted to oppose. King announced that a prevailing majority is in favor of this motion. From my observation there was a unanimous vote affirming acceptance of the resolution and recommendations. Then King informed the people that everything expressed in this meeting was being recorded by our secretary, Rev. Fields and tape recorded by Rev. Glasco.

Acknowledging that preachers have many engagements, King asked Rev. Bennett to preside over the remainder of the meeting because he would have to leave to go and speak to the fathers and sons of the city. He was referring to the YMCA fathers and sons banquet where he had been scheduled to speak that evening. Before leaving, he emphasized the need for raising money to support our effort and said that an offering was being taken tonight. He promised that the money would be well used. King asked Reverend Bonner to come and take the offering. He also asked Nixon and Matthews to assist him in receiving the offering. After consulting with Bonner he said we need ten ministers to collect the money from the hundreds, maybe, thousands of people on the outside. Bonner began calling the names of ministers who would collect money from the people outside. King said, "I am going to leave my offering as I leave and I hope that everyone will continue and give your offering." Just before he left he said, "Reverend Bennett will preside during the remainder of this meeting. I am sorry that I have to leave, but I am certainly happy to see your enthusiasm."

There would not be much more happening in the mass meeting after the offering was collected. King, Abernathy, French, Nixon, Wilson, Bennett and I agreed just as King was on his way out of the building that we would have another mass meeting on Thursday, December 8, at 7:00 p.m., at the St. John AME Church. When King was informed about this meeting he thought that it was a good idea. I made an announcement that informed people of the next mass meeting that will be held on Thursday, December 8, at 7:00 p.m., at St. John AME Church. I also told them that a new organization had been formed and that Rev. King had been elected to be president of this organization, and that they would learn more about this organization and its purpose at the Thursday evening mass meeting. Rev. Wilson expressed thanks to all the people and commended them for the unity that they had expressed. Rev. Bennett pronounced the benediction.

As I drove home I reflected upon a wonderful day that was about to end. Many emotions stirred within my soul. Perhaps the dominant one was joy. Before saying my last prayer that day I said to myself, "What a day!" In a certain way, it had been the day that began the Civil Rights Movement during the most tumultuous period in America since the Civil War. And, its focus was the same issue that had caused the Civil War to be fought. That major issue was injustice for black people in America. I reasoned that this day would live, not "in infamy" as President Franklin D. Roosevelt had said following Japan's December 7, 1941 attack on Pearl Harbor, but that this day, December 5, 1955 would live "famously" and be remembered as such by black people in Montgomery and by others who will learn about what happened here on this day, including those yet unborn.

The second day of the boycott brought people of Montgomery face to face with a new reality: black people had launched an attack on the way white folk unilaterally, without input from blacks, decided what was best for blacks or, if not best, what they would have or not have. Black people in Montgomery were fed-up with acquiescing to white oppression, and the bus boycott was their way of demonstrating their disdain and resolve to change things. Black leaders had received a mandate from black Montgomerians to bring about a change in the way black bus riders were treated. But this was about more than the mistreatment of black bus riders. It was about justice for black people. Black leaders were under no illusion. They realized that the road ahead would be difficult as they pursued an untrodden path of conducting a bus boycott and negotiating justice in bus transportation in Montgomery. The eight-day long bus boycott led by Rev. Theodore Jemison in Baton Rouge nearly two years earlier did not offer any real encouragement. It had ended without changing the way black bus riders were treated, certainly without ending bus segregation. There was a high probability that the Montgomery bus boycott would suffer the same fate, and under any circumstance it would be an ordeal for black people. But among most blacks, their leaders in particular, it was a cause worth fighting for, worth paying for, however great the price. King even said in other words it is worth dying for. This was a day for reflection, a time for leaders to gaze upon the future and seek divine guidance from the God whom many of them professed to have a personal relationship with and trusted to provide whatever resources they needed, including directing them in fighting for freedom, justice and equality.

Mid-morning that day King met at Attorney Gray's office to explain to the news media the demands the MIA had made on the city and bus company officials. He gave particular attention to the request for a first-come, first-serve policy and he emphasized that blacks were not asking for an end to segregation. He also expressed the view that we were not addressing segregation per se because that was a matter for the legislature and the courts. "All we are seeking," he said, "is justice and fair treatment for black bus riders." Following the news conference, seven of the black leaders who attended the conference discussed privately the agenda for the first executive board meeting that would be held the next day. We also shared with each other our feelings and thoughts about the outpouring of enthusiasm that had occurred the day before and our anxieties. I told King that I would call the members of the executive board and remind them to be present and on time for the executive board meeting. He thought that was a good thing to do.

At 10:00 a.m., on Wednesday, the members of the executive board met to determine what committees we needed, how we should proceed in achieving our objectives and the addition of new members to the executive board. Two of the eighteen persons who had been selected at the organizing meeting to serve on the executive board decided that they did not want to serve on the board. One of them felt that being a board member could jeopardize his job. The other person gave a health problem as the reason she had decided not to serve on the board. King suggested that we consider adding the additional nine members needed to complete the twenty-five member executive board at a later date so that we could give our time to determining how we might begin negotiating with city and bus company officials. At this point these officials had refused to negotiate or indicate a willingness to do so. There was a consensus during the board meeting that we should make contact with white clergymen to see if we could get their support in resolving the conflict.

We had received word while in our meeting that the semi-annual meeting of the board of the Alabama Council on Human Relations (ACHR) was taking place in Montgomery, and that a board member of that organization, Thomas R. Thrasher, a Montgomery pastor, and Executive Director Robert E. Hughes were trying to persuade city and bus company officials to begin negotiating with black leaders as the best approach to end the boycott. The Mayor had already said that he would refuse to meet with law-breaking black leaders who were acting in violation of the laws of Alabama by conducting a boycott of city buses. That afternoon ACHR executive Director Hughes and Thrasher called city officials, James H. Bagley and Jack Crenshaw from Montgomery City Lines with the request that they meet with black leaders. They were told by them that they were just "obeying the law," and indicated that they could not take any position different from the one that they had expressed publicly. Later Thrasher contacted Mayor Gayle, a member of his church, and expressed to him his frustration with the lack of communication between city officials and black leaders. Mayor Gayle suggested that a meeting be called for Thursday morning. When Hughes called King to inform him about the meeting, King accepted. King then called Abernathy and the other members of the MIA's negotiating team and apprized them of the meeting that they were to have with city officials on tomorrow morning.

On Thursday, December 9, at 10:00 a.m., King, Abernathy, Gray, Robinson, Wilson, myself and three other persons representing the MIA met with the three city commissioners, Gayle, Sellers and Parks, several attorneys who represented the city and Bagley and Crenshaw who represented the bus company. The Mayor wanted to know what did we, black leaders, want to say. King stated that the MIA proposed courteous treatment by bus drivers; seating on a first-come, first-serve basis, with blacks seated from rear to front, whites from front to rear; and employment of black bus drivers on predominately black bus routes. Crenshaw was the main spokesman for the bus company and, in a certain way, for the city commissioners, who chose to have little to say. He said that he had no problem with bus drivers being courteous to all bus riders. Obviously, that request, while well intended, when expressed in a verbal or written agreement it can be nebulous. Crenshaw objected to the MIA's seating plan. And while he didn't say it at that meeting, he later stated that "the MIA's plan would mean that a Negro man could be practically rubbing knees with a white woman." After about two hours of wrangling, Mayor Gayle called for a halt to the proceedings and asked that a smaller group, King and Gray, Sellers and Parks, Bagley and Crenshaw, discuss the matter privately. No progress was made in the smaller group after another two hours. Neither side expressed a willingness to change its position. Four hours of unproductive discussion was all that was accomplished or could be said about the first negotiating meeting.

After the meeting, the MIA leaders wired this letter to the National City Lines in Chicago, owner of the Montgomery bus franchise:

To The National City Lines, Inc.
616 South Michigan Ave., Chicago, Ill.

Over a period of years the Negro passengers on the Montgomery City Lines, Inc., have been subjected to humiliation, threats, intimidation, and death through bus driver action.

The Negro has been inconvenienced in the use of the city bus lines by the operators in all instances in which the bus has been crowded. He has been forced to give up his seat if a white person has been standing.

Repeated conferences with the bus officials have met with failure. Today a meeting was held with Mr. J. H. Bagley and Attorney Jack Crenshaw as representatives of the bus company and Mayor W. A. Gayle and Associate Commissioners Frank Parks and Clyde Sellers. At which time as an attempt to end the Monday through Thursday protest, the following three proposals were made:

1. Courteous treatment by bus drivers.

2. Seating of Negro passengers from rear to front of bus, and white passengers from front to rear on a "first-come-first-served basis" with no seats reserved for any race.

3. Employment of Negro bus operators in predominantly Negro residential sections.

The above proposals, and the resolutions which will follow, were drafted and adopted in a mass meeting of more than 5,000 regular bus riders. These proposals were denied in the meeting with the city officials and representatives of the bus company.

Since 44% of the city's population is Negro, and since 75% of the bus riders are Negro, we urge you to send a representative to Montgomery to arbitrate.

The Montgomery Improvement Association
The Rev. M. L. King, President
The Rev. U. J. Fields, Secretary

On that Thursday night, the MIA held its second mass meeting at the St. John AME Church. The establishment of a car pool to meet the transportation needs of bus boycotters was at the top of the agenda. It was felt that the car pool system could be patterned after the "Operation Free Lift" car pool that Jemison had during the bus boycott in Baton Rouge. It was noted that our car pool could not operate free of charge to those using it. Attendees at the mass meeting again expressed their support for their leaders and satisfaction with the position they had taken during the first negotiating session with city and bus line officials.

The following day the Montgomery City Lines announced that it would cut bus service in most "Negro districts," effective 6:00 p.m., on December 10 and a city official said that the city would enforce a minimum fare for cabs. This was a move aimed at preventing black taxicabs from charging less than the legal minimum fare to black cab riders. Also on that same day the MIA released a "Statement of Negroes on Bus Segregation" that indicated that the bus company could accept the MIA's seating proposal without breaking Alabama's segregation laws. The statement gave the MIA's position on the Alabama Stature requiring segregation, as found in the Act of July 18, 1947, (General Acts of Alabama, 1947, #130, Page 40) which we held authorized such a policy but did not require it. The statement said in part:

The Legislature, it seems clear, wisely left it up to the transportation companies to work out the seating problem in a reasonable and practical way, subject to the limitations of reasonableness and equality of treatment to all passengers, regardless of race.

It should be further noted that even under the City Code of Montgomery (Chapter 6, Section 10 and 11) no person, white or colored, can be required to give up a seat unless there is a vacant seat in the portion of the bus to which the passenger is assigned.

The statement concluded with these words:

We feel that there is no issue between the Negro citizens and the Montgomery City Lines that cannot be solved by negotiations between people of good will and we submit that there is no legal barrier to such negotiations."
Respectfully submitted,
The Montgomery Improvement Association

M. L. King, President
U. J. Fields, Secretary
T.D.RGP.

During our drafting of the aforementioned letter I strongly objected to the content of the letter, mainly because it was an endorsement or acceptance of the acceptability of segregation. However, my objection was overruled by the majority approval of the letter in the form which it appears above.

On Monday, December 12, marking the first week of the boycott, the third mass meeting was held at the Bethel Baptist Church. The people attending the meeting were informed that an organized car pool would begin operation on the following day. Some locations were announced where people would be picked-up and dispatched, including the time for boarding these cars. The following day King, Gray and Rosa Parks met with W. C. Patton, state field secretary for the NAACP. Patton was told by King and Gray that the MIA's ultimate goals were the same as the NAACP but that they were working to solve some immediate crisis in Montgomery that justified them making the demands they had made on city officials, including the first-come, first-serve seating plan, The NAACP had some concern as to whether the MIA's seating plan would be contributing to maintaining segregation on buses. Patton said in his report to Executive Secretary Roy Wilkins that "the MIA's present plan is a tentative plan aimed at dealing with bus segregation in Montgomery. It appeared that the MIA's ultimate goals were the same as the NAACP's," he concluded.

Montgomery Police Chief G. J. Ruppenthal ordered strict enforcement of a city law prohibiting more than three people in the front seat of passenger cars and said that cab drivers charging less than the forty-five cents per passenger would be prosecuted to the full extent of the law. He had heard that black taxicab drivers were charging only ten or fifteen cents per passenger.

On Wednesday, December 14, the executive board held its second meeting. Much of the discussion focused on making the car pool more effective. Some people still did not have access to the car pool. Rufus A. Lewis said that some 215 persons had already volunteered to be drivers in the car pool. He saw setting up the "pick-up and dispatch" stations as being the most urgent need. During that meeting Rev. R. J. Glasco, director of the Alabama Negro Baptist Center and Rev. A. W. Wilson, a trustee of the Baptist Center and the black minister with the strongest connection with white Southern Alabama Baptist in Montgomery felt that since the boycott was lasting a while longer than all of us had expected, the MIA should consider moving it's headquarters from the Baptist Center to another location. He noted that the Southern Baptist made financial contributions toward the missions program and training ministries of the Baptist Center and that some of their representatives from the white Montgomery Baptist Association had expressed concern about the Baptist Center housing the MIA's headquarters. The members of the executive board voted, without debate, to move the MIA's headquarters to Rufus Lewis's Citizen Club.

On Thursday, December 15, Kenneth E. Totten, a representative of National City Lines, arrived in Montgomery, and said that he was interested in talking with any group anxious to discuss the boycott, at least that is what was reported in the news. Although he met with Mayor Gayle, City Commissioners Frank Parks and Clyde Sellers, on the following day he made no effort to meet with any MIA official. King and other black leaders were perturbed that the bus company's national representative made no effort to speak with MIA leaders, even though we had wired a communication to National City Lines six days before asking that we meet with one of the company's representatives.

That night the mass meeting was held at the First Baptist Church. Lewis, chairman of the MIA's Transportation Committee, reported that all had gone well during the first three days of the car pool. He said some 215 volunteer drivers had already participated, and that the "pick-up and dispatch stations system"—some of them at black churches (one was at the Bell Street Baptist Church where I was the pastor)—had proved effective. During much of his talk, King focused on the White Citizens Council that had received a lot of support, financial and "immoral," from the white community and an unusual amount of coverage in the news media. He contrasted the views of the White Citizens Council with those of the MIA, noting that they are for hate and violence while we are for justice and love. It was announced that the MIA headquarters would move to the

Citizens Club effective on Monday.

Late Friday, Thrasher and Hughes of the ACHR set up a second meeting for all the parties involved in the negotiation for Saturday morning at the Chamber of Commerce. Mayor Gayle invited a number of representatives from the white community to attend the meeting. During the Saturday meeting, discussion was focused on Montgomery adopting a plan similar to the bus plan that was currently in effect in Mobile that was more liberal and respectful of black bus riders. King stated that the MIA was no longer asking that the bus company hire Negro drivers immediately. Crenshaw reiterated his previous plan, and refused to admit that there was a problem with the plan now employed by the bus company. Totten agreed. Totten's remarks coming before he had any conversation with the MIA, infuriated King and the rest of the members of his committee. Several members of Gayle's group spoke, including G. Stanley Frazer, minister of St. James Methodist Church. He gave some paternalistic remarks, stating that ministers should stay out of politics. King responded, noting that he sees no conflict between our devotion to Jesus Christ and our present action. He also asked this question: "Where are the black politicians in this city?" That was a question that no white person at the meeting dared to answer because there was not a singe black politician in Montgomery.

The Rev. Henry Parker of the white First Baptist Church attempted to bridge the substantive differences which would prove to be as difficult for him as making apples into oranges. He felt that the problem was that Negro passengers do not know where the reserved section for whites ends and proposed putting up signs on buses. MIA leaders objected in unison to "White Only" signs, which had been eliminated from Montgomery buses twenty years earlier. At that point some whites threatened to end the meeting if it could not be conducted orderly. Rev. Parker proved that he could not so much as identify the problem, let alone contribute to its solution. For bus riders there had not been a time when the signs, whether posted or not posted, were not visible to the "psyche" sights of black and white bus riders.

Gayle then moved to appoint a small citizen's committee to discuss the issue and report back to the city commissioners. He named eight of the whites already in attendance plus two blacks not connected to the MIA, who were seen as suspects by other blacks present. He offered the MIA three representatives on the committee, but Jo Ann Robinson immediately broke in, stating that if the committee had eight whites, it should have eight blacks. Gayle conceded to the point, and eight MIA leaders—King, Abernathy, Robinson, Fields, Wilson, Hubbard and attorneys Gray and Langford—joined the eight whites and two alleged suspect "Uncle Toms"—P. M. Blair and Dungee Caffey, as the other participants departed. I knew both Blair and Caffey, the former better than the latter. Blair had a dry cleaning business, located almost directly across the street from Abernathy's parsonage and Caffey was also a businessman, but blacks were of the opinion that he was merely a front man for whites who owned the businesses he claimed to be his own. I did not feel that Blair was on the mayor's side of the issue but that he wanted to gain some power to satisfy his ego so he could make blacks feel that he was a leader. I could not make up my mind about Caffey. My guess was that he leaned considerably in the direction of being an "Uncle Tom." They both should have known that the mayor was not up to any good insofar as dealing justly with blacks engaged in the bus protest. That was obvious to anyone in Montgomery who had eyes to see and ears to hear. Even whites knew that, but they were counting on the mayor to maintain the status quo. The mayor had done nothing since the boycott began that would indicate that he wanted to deal justly with blacks. And besides, it would seem to me that the known black leaders should have been allowed to select their own representatives.

The smaller committee was able to agree upon a resolution calling for everyone on the bus to be courteous to others, but made no other headway. The white members offered a resolution that deadlocked in the committee. It called for blacks to postpone the boycott until January 15. Some whites talked about the Christmas spirit and the significance of the season for Christians in an attempt to soften black folk's wills. They even mentioned that this was the time of year for "peace and goodwill." But it did not work. The meeting adjourned, having not accomplished anything. Blacks on that committee, like other blacks, realized that whites in Montgomery should be the last people on earth to talk about the Christmas spirit in a Christian context since their behavior toward blacks was anything but

Christian. They consistently coped-out of doing justly in the name of "obeying the law" that they or their kind had instituted for the purpose of denying blacks justice. Many Nazis said the same thing in offering justification for their participation in the holocaust that purportedly killed six million Jews.

It was Monday, December 19, just six days before Christmas, and the black folk in Montgomery were not waiting on Santa Claus to come to town or planning to do much shopping for Christmas. While a decrease in the usual amount of Christmas shopping by black people would not impact the stores as much as blacks' boycotting buses impacted the Montgomery City Lines, white businessmen did anticipate a decrease of some significance in their profits that Christmas. Some Montgomery retailers, as did some city officials, called upon whites to spend more money that Christmas to make up for the decrease in the amount of money blacks were expected not to spend that Christmas.

This was the day the mayor's special "citizens" committee met. The committee members arrived at the Chamber of Commerce office at 9:00 a.m. No sooner than the committee was called to order, Gray informed King that a newcomer to the committee was Luther Ingalls, secretary of the Montgomery White Citizens Council. When Ingalls started to speak, King questioned his role. Although I had seen him on television it never occurred to me that he was a White Citizens Council official until King questioned his presence in the meeting. Committee Chairman Parker explained that Gayle had added him to the group, and that a white member now would become a nonvoting secretary. King said the mayor had acted unfairly by adding him to the committee without consulting the MIA representatives. King went on to say that some whites had preconceived ideas. His statement about members having "preconceived ideas," got the attention of some whites on the committee. Mrs. Logan A. Hipp told King, "I resent very deeply the statement that we have come here with preconceived ideas. I most certainly did not." Her statement seemed to have been made to deflect attention away from the matter of Ingalls being on the committee. Abernathy spoke after listening to several white folk express their dissatisfaction about what King had said. Focusing on what one of them said about not believing that other MIA representatives felt the same way as King, Abernathy said, "King is speaking, not just for himself, as you have charged, but for all black representatives." King made a motion for a recess. After a contentions meeting, the mayor adjourned the meeting with no plans for another session.

That evening, King presided over the mass meeting that was held at the Hutchinson Street Baptist Church. He stated that two negotiating meetings had been held with the mayor and other city officials and MIA representatives, but that they had both been unproductive. "Whites," he said, "had not shown a willingness to act in good faith. Instead, they have insisted that we drop our demands and go back to riding the buses. They have not as yet considered our demands as being legitimate." He added, "plans are being made for a twelve-month bus protest, if necessary."

On Thursday, December 12, the MIA executive board met in a lengthy four and one-half hour meeting where we discussed the city officials' failure to make a positive response to our demands. Members of the board agreed that our demands were legitimate, even though city officials had not acknowledged them as being legitimate. King stated that we were as far away from any deal in settling the protest as we were on the first day of the boycott. He predicted that if we continue the protest we would see a victory, maybe not tomorrow or next week, but in the non-too distant future. We then discussed how we might present our story to the Montgomery people, both black and white. After some discussion on that matter it was agreed that we should take out a paid advertisement in the *Montgomery Advertiser* that would present the facts and clarify the issues surrounding the boycott from our perspective. We were hopeful that we could have it published on the day after Christmas. Members appointed to serve on the Publicity Committee were: Robinson, Abernathy, French, Pierce and myself. King would serve as an ex-officio member of the committee. We agreed that our statement to the Montgomery public would represent the diversity in the city's black leadership, not just that of the MIA. King urged all board members to be present for the mass meeting that would be held that evening. The meeting adjourned.

Although King, Abernathy and French contributed significantly in preparing this statement, "To the Montgomery Public," particularly, in terms of determining its content, it was Robinson,

Pierce and myself who contributed most in its formulation. Robinson and Pierce had been my teachers about a year earlier when I was in undergraduate school at Alabama State College. I had studied English literature under Robinson, a course that seemed to be more like writing, telling stories and news reporting, than English. She was an excellent teacher. Pierce had taught me Political Science. He was born in Lowndes County, a rural county that joined Montgomery County. At the beginning of the bus boycott there was not a single registered black voter in Lowndes County where the majority of the population was black. Pierce had received his B. S. degree from the University of Toledo and his M. S. degree from Ohio State University and returned in the early 1930s to his native state to teach at Alabama State College. Unlike Robinson who was gentle and diplomatic in her manners, Pierce was angry and bitter when segregation or white racism was the issue. He suffered as a teacher at Alabama State College because he could not express his rage overtly in fighting white racism, that is, if he wanted to keep his job. Even the things that Robinson did politically Pierce could not have done and survived as a teacher, maybe not even as a person. Black women have been permitted by the white man, with no credit due the white man, to behave in ways contrary to the white man's plans or expectations for them without having to suffer as much for their actions as black men who behaved similarly. Pierce, now sixty years old, had already helped in the development of a generation of black minds. Some of his students had become emboldened human rights activists. When Pierce, Robinson and I worked on "To the Montgomery Public," including one night until after midnight, "burning the midnight oil," so to speak, I jokingly said to them, "Now all three of us are 'burning the midnight oil' just as I had to do when I was your student." Following is the statement that appeared in a half-page advertisement in the Sunday *Montgomery Advertiser*:

To the Montgomery Public
December 25, 1955
Montgomery, Ala.

We, the Negro citizens of Montgomery, feel that the public has a right to know our complaints and grievances which have resulted in the protest against Montgomery City Lines and our refusal to ride city buses. We, therefore, set forth here some of the many bitter experiences of our people, who have at various times, been pushed around, embarrassed, threatened, intimidated and abused in a manner that has caused the meekest to rise in resentment:

COMPLAINTS:

1. *Courtesy:*

The use of abusive language, name calling and threats have been the common practices among many of the bus operators. We are ordered to move from seats to standing space under the threat of arrest, or other serious consequences. No regard for sex or age is considered in exercising this authority by the bus operator.

2. *Seating:*

The bus operators have not been fair in this respect. Negroes, old, young, men and women, mothers with babes in their arms, sick, afflicted, pregnant women, must relinquish their seats, even to school children, if the bus is crowded. On lines serving predominantly Negro sections, the ten front seats must remain vacant, even though no white passenger boards the bus. At all times the Negro is asked to give up his seat, though there is not standing room in the back. One white person, desiring a seat, will cause nine Negroes to relinquish their seats for the accommodation of this one person.

3. *Arrests:*

Numerous arrests have been made even though the person arrested is observing the policy as given us. This year the following persons have been arrested and convicted, although they were seated according to the policy given us by the bus company. They are Claudette Colvin, Alberta "Coote" Smith and Rosa Parks. Among others arrested at other times are Viola White, Mary Wingfield, two children from New Jersey and R. Brooks, who was killed by a policeman.

4. *Two Fares:*

Many house-servants are required to pay an additional fare if the bus is late getting to town, causing them to miss a bus going to Cloverdale or other distant points. Some of these have complained that on returning from work similar incidents have occurred necessitating the payment of double fares.

5. *Making Change:*

We understand that correct change should be given the operator, but there are times that such is not possible. Several bus operators have refused to make change for passengers and threatened to put them off the bus for not having the exact amount. On one occasion a fellow-passenger paid the fare of one such passenger to prevent her from being put off.

6. Passing Up Passengers:

In many instances the bus operators have passed up passengers standing at the stop to board the bus. They have also collected fares at the front door and, after commanding Negro passengers to enter from the back door, they have driven off, leaving them standing.

7. Physical Torture:

One Negro mother, with two small children in her arms, put them on the front seat while she opened her purse for her fare. The driver ordered her to take the children from the seat, and without giving her the chance to place the children elsewhere, lunged the vehicle forward, causing the small children to be thrown into the aisle of the bus.

8. Acknowledgment:

Not all operators are guilty of these accusations. There are some who are most cordial and tolerant. They will go to the extent of their authority to see that justice and fair play prevail. To those we are grateful and sympathetic.

9. Adjudication

Every effort has been used to get the bus company to remove the causes of these complaints. Time and time again complaints have been registered with the bus company, the City Commission and the manager of the bus company. Committees of both sexes have been conferred but to no avail. Protest have been filed with the mayor, but no improvement has been made.

In March we held a conference with the Manager of the Montgomery City Lines and made a very modest request (1) that the bus company attorney meet with our attorneys and give an interpretation to laws regulating passengers and (2) that the policy of the bus on seating be published so that all bus riders would be well-informed on the policy of the bus. To this date this has not been done.

The manager read to us the city code and informed us that this is in the hands of every bus driver. At this meeting, the arresting officers of Claudette Colvin case were there along with the Police Commissioner. The bus operator, who caused the arrest of Claudette Colvin, was requested to be present, but did not come.

A committee met with the Mayor and an Associate Commissioner when the bus company requested a raise in fare. No protest was made against the raise, but only against seating and courteous treatment of passengers. Nothing came of this and Negroes were treated worse after the increase in bus fare than before.

The Great Decision:

The bus protest is not merely in protest of the arrest of Rosa Parks, but is the culmination of a series of unpleasant incidents over a period of years. It is an upsurging of a groundswell which has been going on for a long time. Our cup of tolerance has run over. Thousands of our people, who have had unhappy experiences, prefer to walk rather than endure more. No better evidence can be given than the fact that a large percent of the Negro bus riders are now walking or getting a ride whenever and wherever they can.

Our Proposal:

The duly elected representatives of the people have the approval of the bus riders to present three proposals:

1. That assurance of more courtesy be extended the bus-riders. That the bus operators refrain from name calling, abusive language and threats.

2. That the seating of passengers will be on a "First-come, First-served" basis. This means that the Negro passengers will begin seating from the rear of the bus toward the front and white passengers from the front toward the rear, until all seats are taken. Once seated, no passenger will be compelled to relinquish his seat to a member of another race when there is no available seat. When seats become vacant in the rear Negro passengers will voluntarily move to these vacant seats and by the same token white passengers will move to vacant seats in the front of the bus. This will eliminate the problem of passengers being compelled to stand when there are unoccupied seats. At no time, on the basis of this proposal, will both races occupy the same seat. We are convinced by the opinions of competent legal authorities that this proposal does not necessitate a change in the city, or state laws. This proposal is not new in

Alabama, for it has worked for a number of years in Mobile and many other Southern cities.

3. That Negro bus drivers be employed on the bus lines serving predominantly Negro areas. This is a fair request and we believe that men of goodwill will readily accept it and admit that it is fair.

Nature of Movement:

1. Non violence–

At no time have the participants of this movement advocated or anticipated violence. We stand willing and ready to report and give any assistance in exposing persons who resort to violence. This is a movement of passive resistance, depending on moral and spiritual forces. We, the oppressed, have no hate in our hearts for the oppressors, but we are, nevertheless, determined to resist until the cause of justice triumphs.

2. Coercion--

There has not been any coercion on the part of any leader to force anyone to stay off the buses. The rising tide of resentment has come to fruition. This resentment has resulted in a vast majority of the people staying off the buses willingly and voluntarily.

3. Arbitration--

We are willing to arbitrate. We feel that this can be done with men and women of goodwill. However, we find it rather difficult to arbitrate in good faith with those whose public pronouncements are anti-Negro and whose only desire seems to be that of maintaining the status quo. We call upon men of goodwill who will be willing to treat this issue in the spirit of Him whose birth we celebrate at this season, to meet with us. We stand for Christian teachings and the concepts of democracy for which men and women of all races have fought and died.

The Negro Ministers of Montgomery and Their Congregations
The Methodist Ministerial Alliance
The Rev. J. W. Hayes, President
The Baptist Ministers' Conference
The Rev. H. H. Hubbard, President
The Rev. R. D. Abernathy, Secretary
The Interdenominational Ministerial Alliance
The Rev. L. Roy Bennett, President
The Rev. J. C. Parker, Secretary

The Montgomery Improvement Association
Dr. M. L. King, Jr., President
The Rev. U. J. Fields, Secretary

That Thursday night, three days before Christmas Day, a mass meeting was held at the Mt. Zion AME Church. This had been the church where the MIA was founded and organized not quite three weeks earlier. Since the boycott began, our faith had been tested severely. This was a collective truth that many could testify to. During the mass meeting people were told to be sure to read the MIA's statement, "To the Montgomery Public," that would appear in the Sunday's *Montgomery Advertiser* on the day after Christmas. King said that this statement "expressed our views and position on the bus protest." Several leaders expressed the hope that everyone would have a blessed Christmas. Rev. Wilson said, "This Christmas can be wonderful for us if we remember the 'reason for the season' and Whose birthday we are celebrating, despite the boycott and the fact that we will be spending less money shopping than we usually spend at Christmas."

Since that last contentious meeting with the mayor's committee, there had been no communication between city officials and MIA leaders. K. E. Totten had left the city the same day we held our last mass meeting, before Christmas, after expressing the opinion that there was not anything he could contribute in resolving the conflict. That same day the city officials announced that after having reduced the number of routes in service, the cancellation of all bus service for several days over the Christmas–New Year's period. A spokesman for the city said that the small number of bus riders might make it necessary to significantly increase a bus fare in 1956, but would not say what amount that would be.

On Monday, December 26, the day after Christmas and the day our statement "To the Montgomery Public" appeared in the *Montgomery Advertiser*, we held a mass meeting that focused heavily on a discussion of that statement. On Thursday, December 29, another mass meeting was held at Day Street Baptist Church where Rev. M. C. Cleveland was the pastor. He had not indicated any interest in the boycott previously. Both of these mass meetings featured several speakers who gave pep talks. One or more pep talks were given at each mass meeting. They were aimed at encouraging people to "keep-on-keeping-on" and to continue to make it clear in the minds and hearts of the people why we, as a people, dare not end the boycott until we are respected and receive justice.

The people were assured at these last two mass meetings of the year that the car pool would continue to operate during the remainder of the holiday season even though the city had been unable or unwilling to keep the buses running. MIA leaders expressed no regret that the buses ceased operation during the holidays.

On the following day, Mayor Gayle broke his silence and urged Montgomery citizens to patronize city buses or risk losing the bus company's business. He finally agreed with black leaders that the boycott was ninety-five percent effective. The boycott had hit the bus company in the pocketbook, where it hurt most. On the last day of 1955, New Year's Eve, many black people attended night services at various churches. One of these services was held at the Bell Street Baptist Church as had been the practice at this church long before I became the pastor. Most of those attending these services remained at church beyond midnight and witnessed the old year end and the new year begin. Although these twenty-seven days of boycotting buses had been an "ordeal without a deal" most black people in Montgomery rang in the New Year with hope and joy.

The holiday season was over. Although black Montgomerians had not done as much shopping this holiday season as in past holiday seasons, a number of them I talked with had eaten their usual New Year's Day dinner that consisted of fried chicken, mashed potatoes, baked corn (corn pudding), green beans and sweet potatoes. Some had managed to have the New Year's soul food special: hog head cheese, collard greens and black-eye peas. And a few had eaten chitterlings. January 1956 began the fourth week of the bus protest. Our motto was "Going Forward," in spirit, if not in words. Even a sermon King preached on the subject "Going Forward by Going Backward," that challenged his listeners to go backward and claim those values and practices that enabled our African ancestors to achieve great things, was primarily about the future. In that sermon he recited this Scripture several times:

And the Lord said unto Moses,
Wherefore criest thou unto me?
Speak unto the children of Israel,
that they go forward. (Exodus 14:15)

Bus company official Totten had returned to Montgomery from Chicago, but had given no indication that he wanted to meet with black leaders. In New York, NAACP executive director Wilkins instructed W. W. Patton, his representative in Alabama, to inform MIA leaders that the organization could not at present assist in any appeal of Rosa Parks' conviction because of the MIA's seating proposal. The NAACP could not join in "on any basis other than the elimination of segregation seating on the city buses." The organization already was handling a case to desegregate the city buses of Columbia, South Carolina, and could not enter an Alabama case asking merely for, as Wilkins aptly put it, "polite segregation." Montgomery City Lines announced that it was losing twenty-two cents for every mile one of its buses travels, and applied to the city commissioners for a fare increase from ten to twenty cents. The company acknowledged that the bus boycott was ninety-five percent effective.

King, asked for comment, said that the MIA would meet with anyone interested in settling the protest, but he knew of no circumstances in which the three demands would be dropped. Before he made that statement I had talked with him and strongly suggested that we give up our number two demand, maybe all our demands, and ask for integration. He and Gray, who had been listening to our conversation, felt that we should stick to our three demands. On January 4 I expressed, in writing, to the *Montgomery Advertiser* my position from henceforth forward, in this statement: "The Negroes of Montgomery have no desire to compromise regarding the three demands. These demands were nothing more than a compromise to begin with. We should have demanded complete integration, and that is what we want." This was the first time a leader in Montgomery had declared publicly that we wanted desegregation on Montgomery buses. King did not like what I had said, and he attempted to reprimand me, I supposed for two reasons: (1) he was still convinced that we should stay within the segregation laws of Alabama, and (2) he did not want anyone other than himself to voice publicly an opinion of significance on the protest, especially if it was different from his own views. Although King got many of his ideas from Abernathy and Abernathy had no problem using other folk's ideas, sometimes without giving them their due credit, including ideas he got from me, neither Abernathy, Gray or King was ready to switch and advocate integration rather than to continue to embrace what Wilkins' referred to as "polite segregation" on Montgomery buses. Abernathy, Gray, King and I, all born and reared in the South, three of us in Alabama, were accustomed to segregation. We had spent only a limited amount of our lives beyond the Mason-Dixon line. Abernathy had spent a tour of duty in the segregated Army and was exposed to very little integration; Gray had spent three years in the North while attending Ohio's Case Western Reserved University; King had spent about four and a half years while attending Crozier Seminary in Pennsylvania and Boston University in Massachusetts; and I had spent four years in the Army, half of that time in segregated Army units and the other half in integrated Army units and about a half year in Chicago, prior to returning to Alabama. I cannot speak for them, but while serving in the military I made a vow that I would not return to live in the South because of a strong dislike for segregation. However, I broke my vow and like Abernathy, Gray and King, I returned to Alabama. It is not that either of us wanted segregation, but being willing to fight for it at the time apparently was a different matter for Abernathy, Gray and King. From the time I made my statement to the news media calling for integration, I noticed that King's attitude toward me became more formal and distant. He no longer sought to get my signature on official outgoing MIA correspondence as he had done previously and he deliberately withheld information from me that as secretary I had a right to know. On January 5, the City Commissioners granted the bus company half of what it wanted, raising the adult fare to fifteen cents. Of course, the Commissioners did nothing to meet the demands of MIA leaders and the folk they represented.

I was in the second quarter of Graduate School at Alabama State College working on my Master's Degree in Education when I seriously considered dropping out of school. I felt that being a full-time student, including having to write a thesis, alone with being a pastor and the secretary of the MIA were too much of a load for me to carry. Three days before my scheduled termination date I was visited one night by an angel who appeared to me in full angelic presence and said, not once but three times, "Fields, you are directed to remain in school." A week later I selected this title for my thesis: "Community-School Relationships between the Carver High School and the Community it Serves in Montgomery, Alabama."

At the next MIA Executive Board meeting following my decision to remain in school, I informed members of the executive board that I was resigning, effective immediately, as the secretary of the MIA. I explained that I was attending graduate school and that I would not be able to be an effective secretary any longer. Several board members asked me to reconsider my request and not too resign. Rev. Johnson said, "Fields, you are the most emboldened person in the MIA. We need you." Rev. Wilson said, "Fields, you don't miss a thing when you take the minute. That's what we need and you are the person to do that." There were others who spoke highly of me as being not only a good secretary, but a person much needed as a board member. After reaching an agreement that would allow Erna Dungee, the financial secretary, to take the minutes when I or Rev. French, the corresponding secretary, was not present, I withdrew my resignation. During that meeting, I realized more than before that I should shoulder my part of the load in supporting the boycott which was a gigantic undertaking by black Montgomerians. French was spending more and more of his time out-of-the state performing ministry in a national capacity with the AMEZ Church and Nixon, a Pullman porter, was frequently out of the city making his train runs from Montgomery to Chicago and back. King and Abernathy were contributing greatly to the protest, bearing a heavy load, at times neglecting their pastoral responsibilities which displeased some of their members. How could I not contribute my very best? I reasoned that I could do no less than I had done in the past, regardless as to my other responsibilities.

That evening a mass meeting was held at St. John AME Church. King presided at the meeting. He felt that some positive change would soon occur in the hearts and behavior of city commissioners. He acknowledged that he did not have any evidence to support his feeling or thinking about his optimism. Then he added, "This just may be my hope." He also expressed the opinion that the city could not afford to keep on losing money because of the boycott. On Friday, January 6, Montgomery Attorney Fred Ball sent communications to the *Montgomery Advertiser* and to Solicitor William Thetford that said the MIA's boycott of buses violated Alabama's anti-boycott law. That evening 1,200 people gathered at the city auditorium for a White Citizens Council rally. During the program City Police Commissioner Clyde Sellers came to the podium and announced that he was joining the racist group which blacks considered to be the new KKK. The *Montgomery Advertiser* noted that "in effect, the Montgomery police force is now an arm of the White Citizens Council."

uniting of opposition, not just the oppressed

With new threats of violence being posed by the activity of the White Citizens Council, King contacted Gayle and asked for a meeting between city officials and MIA representatives. He felt that blacks were defenseless against the racist White Citizens Council. On Monday, January 9, the MIA leaders met with city officials. King again emphasized that the objective of the MIA was not to abolish segregation. But Gayle maintained that the city would enforce the law and urged King to call off the boycott. He added, "perhaps then we can talk." The two-hour meeting resolved nothing. Later that evening at a mass meeting at the Bethel Baptist Church, King informed the people of the city officials' unwillingness to respond in any positive way to our demands. He said nothing had changed insofar as resolving the issue that had caused us to protest. Later that week, Reverend Robert Graetz, the white pastor of a black Lutheran congregation and the only visible white activist in the boycott, had his car vandalized. A note was left on his car warning him that he must leave town and be aware that next time it will not be his car, but his life.

On January 10, the Louisville and Nashville Railroad complied with an Interstate Commerce Commission order to end segregation in airline, railroad, and bus terminals serving interstate passengers, and removed signs enforcing segregation from all of its terminals in Alabama. The following day Police Commissioner Sellers, at the request of Circuit Solicitor William F. Thetford, initiated an investigation of the Montgomery movement. Police Chief Ruppenthal delivered the copies of Montgomery city ordinances to managers of bus and train stations requiring segregation facilities. As for Montgomery, nothing had changed. But black leaders, as did white leaders, could see the handwriting on the wall. Change would come even in Montgomery. This was the hope that bus protesters kept alive.

The executive board of the MIA met on Thursday, January 12. After giving some attention to the city's refusal to make any overtures, insofar as granting our requests, we decided that from here on it would be a test of endurance, as to who could hold out the longest time. We again affirmed that we would continue the boycott of buses indefinitely. We also decided to hold a general mass meeting every Monday and three mass meetings every Thursday night in different areas of the city so that it would be convenient for more people to attend the meetings. This would make it possible to give recognition to more ministers and use small churches. This was also our way of digging in for the long haul.

In his press statement on January 15, King conceded to reporters that the MIA's seating proposal was modest and had not won favor with the NAACP. He agreed with a statement I had released earlier to the *Montgomery Advertiser*, which said, "We began with a compromise when we didn't ask for complete integration." This would be the first time that King would acknowledge publicly that he was for integration. At the Monday night mass meeting, King commented further on his favoring integration while maintaining that we were seeking only that our three demands be met as the requirement for ending the protest. He also announced that in the future the MIA would hold a general mass meeting every Monday and three mass meetings every Thursday night in different areas of the city so that it will be more convenient for more people to attend these mass meetings. However, he did not mention that another reason why we decided to have multiple mass meetings on Thursdays was to respond to the complaining of some ministers of smaller congregations who felt that they and their churches were not receiving proper recognition. The people attending the mass meeting did not appear to be enthusiastic about having multiple mass meetings. Nevertheless, we proceeded to have three mass meetings each Thursday and a general mass meeting each Monday.

Grover Hall, Jr., the editor of the *Montgomery Advertiser* wanted to find out who was really furnishing the leadership for the bus boycott. There was a general feeling among many whites and, I must confess, some blacks, that a white person or persons had to be providing leadership for the protest. How else, they reasoned, could it stand up to white power or last as long? Many white people felt that the blacks were not smart enough, wise enough, sophisticated enough, or courageous enough to challenge, let alone change the white man's lifestyle in any significant area of life. Although Hall was considered by some black people to be a moderate segregationist I saw no demonstration, on his part, of him having assisted black folk in their endeavor to receive justice in Montgomery. He permitted whites with non-racist views to express their opinions in his newspaper, but not to the extent that the racist views were expressed. And although he carried the views of moderate blacks he did not, as far as I could determine, carry the views of blacks attacking racism in his newspaper. That included refusing to publish one of my articles.

In his endeavor to find the leader of the boycott, Hall gave that assignment to one of his young reporters named Thomas Johnson. On January 19, Johnson's article titled, "The Rev. King is Boycott Boss," appeared in the *Montgomery Advertiser*. This article caused some people to accept the fact that King was the leader of the boycott. Hall admitted that he had assumed that Graetz or some other white person was the true leader of the boycott. Johnson had even interviewed Graetz earlier and written his first article in the series about him before writing the article announcing that King was "Boss of the Boycott." This further suggests that Johnson, like his boss, felt that Graetz was the real leader of the boycott. Graetz, like a number of other ministers in Montgomery, was a team player and a fellow-sufferer, but none of us on that team ever suspected that he was leader of the boycott. Of course, he was highly committed to the protest, but like other boycott leaders very pleased to not be the chief leader of the boycott. Black leaders as well as most black people knew that King was the chief leader because they had made him the chief leader.

On Saturday, January 21, after the Mayor's unsuccessful endeavor to get MIA leaders to give up on their demands and return to riding the buses, he contacted three little-known preachers who pastored small churches in Montgomery and invited them to a meeting. These ministers were not actively involved in the MIA. Following that meeting that involved the Mayor's committee and these three invited preachers, the *Montgomery Advertiser* received the story that Saturday night, and the wire press service began distributing the story of the Montgomery Bus Boycott settlement. The "Minneapolis Tribune" reporter Carl T. Rowan, who had visited Montgomery two weeks earlier and was in the process of writing a story on the movement in Montgomery, was a bit puzzled by the settlement terms and the fact that no names were given. Rowan called King in Montgomery and later he talked with Gray. Neither of them had met with the Mayor or knew anything about a meeting that ministers had held with the Major on Saturday. Rowan then contacted Montgomery Police Commissioner Sellers, as King had requested of him, who conceded that the representatives who met with them may not have been members of the MIA. Rowan called King back and informed him of Sellers' comments and apprized him of the urgent need there is for him to warn the black community of the falsity of the city's claim.

Abernathy called to inform me of what had happened. He asked me to call as many ministers as I could and inform them of what had happened and to let them know that the boycott was still on. Immediately, I called King and he told me that Abernathy was correct about the erroneous announcement that was made about the boycott being called off. He said that he did not know who the ministers were who met with the city officials and wanted to know if I had any idea as to who they might be. I told him that I could not think of but one person who might have been involved in the meeting with the Mayor's committee. Then I said, "I don't know whether or not he would have done that." Like Abernathy, King urged me to let the ministers know that the boycott is still on and ask them to make an announcement during their church services and let their members know that the boycott is still on. On Sunday we were able to identify the three ministers who met with the Mayor's committee. They were: Rev. Benjamin F. Mosley, pastor of the First Presbyterian Church, Rev. William Kind, pastor of the Jackson Street Baptist Church (located on the same street as and near King's parsonage) and Bishop Doc. C. Rice, pastor of the AOH Oak Street Holiness Church. I had only heard of, but never met, Rev. Mosley. I knew Kind and Rice quite well. As a matter of fact, I had preached in both of their churches. Kind and Rice definitely were not politically inclined, in my opinion. All three of these men denied that they had made any agreement with the Mayor's committee to end the boycott. A denial in their names was issued to the press. This is the MIA press release that was made the next morning:

You have probably received a statement released from Commissioner Clyde Sellers stating that the Montgomery bus protest is nearing an end as a result of a meeting with a group of Negro ministers, City bus line officials, and the city Commission. If this release gives the impression that an agreement has been reached, it is totally erroneous. If there were any ministers in a meeting with the city Commissioners Saturday, I assure you that they do not represent even a modicum of the Negro bus riders. More than ninety percent of Negroes are not planning to return to riding the buses. The bus protest is still on and will last until our proposals are given sympathetic consideration through our appointed leaders.

The Montgomery Improvement Association
Rev. M. L. King, Jr., President
Rev. U. J. Fields, Secretary

On Monday, January 23, members of the executive board met. The focus of the meeting was on the ministers who had met with the Mayor on last Saturday and the alleged bus settlement agreement. Although the presence of all three of these ministers who had met with the Mayor's committee had been requested, only Rev. Kind attended. He said the Mayor had called him and asked him to meet at the Chamber of Commerce building to discuss an insurance plan that was being considered for adoption by the city. He said the only person he recognized at the meeting was Bishop Rice. He said he asked why the leaders of the MIA were not present and was told that they would not compromise. The meeting, he said, ended with no agreement. Members of the board did not accept Rev. Kind's statement or explanation. They all agreed that these three ministers had done wrong by attending the Mayor's committee meeting. Even Rev. Kind admitted that he had done wrong and asked for forgiveness. Some members suggested that we take some action against them such as encouraging their parishioners to oust them from their pulpits. Rev. Wilson and I were the only voices raised in their behalf. We asked for reconciliation and suggested that we forgive them. Although all members were not convinced that we should forgive them, a majority of the board members joined with Rev. Wilson and me in calling for reconciliation rather than retaliation. King acknowledged that Kind had asked for forgiveness and said, "We can't hurt Uncle Toms by violence, but only by mass action." What made it difficult for some board members to forgive these three ministers was the fact that they had only, at best, invisibly supported the boycott.

After Kind was excused, a heated discussion ensued as to whether or not the MIA should relinquish our number three goal that demanded employment of Negro bus drivers. The reasoning by some members being that if we ceased asking for the employment of Negro bus drivers we would more likely be able to reach a settlement with the city officials. Ronald R. Young, an ex-marine and coach at the St. Jude's Educational Institution, a white owned and controlled Catholic school (grades one through twelve) that was attended exclusively by black students, vehemently opposed dropping the demand for Negro bus drivers. He felt that this was the most important demand we were making. The majority of the members approved of keeping all three demands even though King favored dropping the number three demand.

Some discussion was devoted to an editorial by Johnson that had appeared in the *Montgomery Advertiser*. Rev. King said the editorial was an attempt to show a split between the MIA and the NAACP. He refuted it. Some members of the board, including Nixon, MIA treasurer, felt that King had given the newspaper some misleading information about the internal affairs of the MIA. King had denied that he knew about the transfer of $5,017 to the Citizens Trust Bank in Atlanta that had been made while he was out of the city. Of course, king had authorized the transfer. Members of the board had unanimously agreed to transfer some MIA funds after our attorneys were worried about legal proceedings against the organization and the boycott. King was hurt by the reactions of Nixon and some other board members. He also appeared to be more fearful than before, partly because threats against his family had increased. He had spoken earlier of the White Citizen Council's pronouncements that advocated the use of violence toward Negroes, if that was what would be needed to return Montgomery to its pre-boycott state. Like King, we all knew that he was a marked man.

King offered his resignation to the MIA board. He expressed the view that someone else among us could lead the organization better than he. He spoke of the value of shared term leadership. At the time, King had only served as president of the MIA for seven weeks, which probably seemed to him like seven years. Frankly, I didn't feel that anyone else in that room wanted to be president of the MIA any more than Rev. Bennett had wanted to be president on the day King was elected to that office. Most board members were concerned that if King resigned, it would show that there was a split in the leadership which would give white people the impression that King no longer had the confidence of black people. We repeat here two statements that were made by Rev. S. S. Seay and Rev. A. W. Wilson during that meeting. After referring to King as the Moses of the people of Montgomery, with tears in his eyes, Seay said, "You are young and well-trained in the spirit. I will drink my portion of this cup, but you can drink of it deeper." Wilson said, "Brother King, I would like to see the boycott continue but if you resign as president we should end the boycott immediately." After most board members pleaded with King to remain the president of the MIA a quietness fell upon us. Young made a motion that was seconded by Rev. Hubbard affirming our full confidence in Dr. King and his leadership as president of the MIA. The motion was unanimously approved. King expressed his thanks for our confidence in him and promised to continue to serve as the MIA president.

Gray was authorized to prepare a final recommendation by next week on the lawsuit that would ask the court to declare that the segregation laws of Alabama that required blacks to be segregated on buses are unconstitutional. We were all somber when we left that meeting. Pessimism was much in evidence. We felt more strongly than at any time before that unless something happened in the courts to change the conditions black bus riders faced in Montgomery, nothing would happen. There was an awareness that this could take a long time in the Federal courts and forever in the Alabama courts.

All three members of the city commission announced that they had joined the local White Citizens Council and Mayor Gayle announced that there would not be anymore discussion with black leaders until the MIA leaders are willing to end the boycott. He urged white women of the city to stop helping their servants by offering them rides to work and suggested that they could do their own housework. He said, "The Negroes are laughing at white people behind their backs. They think it's funny that white people who are opposed to the Negro boycott will act as chauffeurs to Negroes who are boycotting the buses." Commissioner Parks announced that dozens of business employers volunteered to lay off employees who supported the boycott. On Thursday, Rufus Lewis and four other blacks took the first step toward organizing a transit company when they petitioned the city commission for a franchise to operate it. On that same day King left Dexter Avenue Baptist Church in his car with a friend and the church secretary, and after picking up three others at a MIA station, King was arrested, taken to jail, fingerprinted, photographed, and jailed. Later that evening three mass meetings were held, including one at Bell Street Baptist Church. The huge crowds that gathered expressed their concern about King's arrest and the hard-line approach the city officials had taken toward blacks. They all seemed to sense that a new wave of violence was coming.

On Friday, January 27, the MIA, three black ministerial organizations and a civic organization, namely, The Baptist Ministers' Conference, Methodist Ministerial Alliance, Interdenominational Ministerial Alliance, and the Citizens Coordinating Committee, joined with the Montgomery Improvement Association and published a statement titled "To the Citizens of Montgomery" that appeared in the *Montgomery Advertiser*. This was meant to convey a conciliatory message. It read:

Approximately a month ago there was released through these columns a document from the Negro Citizens of Montgomery explaining the reasons the protest had been staged. Since recent public pronouncements have attempted to cloud and distort issues in the protest, we feel that further explanation is needed.

Negroes want the entire citizenry of Montgomery to know that at no time have we raised the race issue in the movement, nor have we directed our aim at the segregation laws. We are interested in a calm and fair consideration of the situation which has developed as a result of dissatisfaction over Bus policies.

The protest, which has been a non-violent method of bargaining, has been used in a democratic society to secure redress of grievances. This technique, however, has caused some of the leaders of the city to inject unrelated issues—such as "destruction of the social fabric" or "the southern tradition," which we feel is an effort to evade the real issue involved.

1. Race Relations: We have used the non-violent approach and have sought relief for our complaints within the framework of the law. We deplore any attempt to pit one race against the other. And we are amazed that there are among us those who could impute any sinister motive other than the request submitted to the Bus Officials and the City Commission. We believe that our proposals, if considered fairly, will help to improve race relations in Montgomery.

2. Democracy: As we interpret the democratic way of life, we are convinced that it gives to each Citizen equal opportunities and privileges to enjoy the benefits of whatever service he is able to pay for, so long as he does not infringe upon the rights of others. Under the present policies to the bus company the rights of Negroes have been infringed upon repeatedly. Up until now our proposals have not been given fair consideration. We have no alternative, therefore, but to continue the bus protest until something fair, just and honorable has been done in our behalf.

3. The Christian Way: We live in a Christian community in which brotherhood and neighborliness should prevail among all the people. We can only rely upon these principles to guide those in authority and other people of influence to see that the Christian way is the only way of reaching a satisfactory solution to the problem.

We submit this to all the Citizens of Montgomery in the name of Him who brought Peace on Earth and Good Will to All Men.

Respectfully submitted,
Negro Ministers and Congregations
Baptist Ministers' Conference
The Rev. H. H. Hubbard, Pres.
Methodist Ministerial Alliance
The Rev. W. J. Hayes, Pres.

Interdenominational Ministerial Alliance
The Rev. L. R. Bennett, Pres.
Citizens Coordinating Committee
Rufus Lewis, Pres.
Montgomery Improvement Association
Dr. M. L. King, Jr., Pres.

The MIA executive board during the January 27 meeting focused on problems Gray was having with the federal suit. Gray had been in communication with Clifford Judkins Durr and NAACP lawyers in New York. All agreed that the federal suit offered the best hope of a court-ordered solution to Montgomery's bus problem. This would be something different from the Rosa Parks' appeal, which was bogged down in state courts. Part of Gray's problem was that of being able to secure plaintiffs who would not back out of the suit, under pressure, that might result in Gray being charged with "barratry," or false legal representation. Durr told him that he knew of a black lawyer who had been driven from the state because of such charges against him. The members of the MIA wanted the federal suit to go forward because if the boycott should end, for whatever reason, without us having had our demands met, then we would not have anything to look forward to and the protest would be seen by most black people as being a failure. All we could do was pray and urge Gray to do his best in the knowledge that he had our full support. The MIA had decided to go the integration way. Gray promised to speed up the process and begin drafting the necessary documents for filing a federal suit.

Following King's sojourn in jail, he read the published statement "To the Citizens of Montgomery," that appeared in the *Montgomery Advertiser*. The executive board met and focused on King's arrest and trial that was to be held the next day. King told us about threats that he continued to receive. Members of the board recommended that King no longer drive himself and that members of the MIA or his church would drive him where he wanted to go and serve as his bodyguards. King did not fully favor that action but accepted it reluctantly and with gratitude. Board members also expressed concern for the safety of other members of King's family. The following day King was fined $14 by recorder's court Judge Luther

H. Waller for speeding, traveling 30 mph in a 25 mph zone.

On Monday, January 30, the executive board met and voted to proceed with the federal suit against segregation in Montgomery. This was not a unanimous vote. There were several board members who strongly favored the MIA continuing its present course of action, i.e. negotiating with the city and bus line officials in the hope that some or all of our demands would be met. But the majority of the board members gave their final approval to Gray filing a federal suit challenging segregation on Montgomery buses. It was agreed that the lawyers be paid $500 for the services they had already rendered.

That night a mass meeting was held at First Baptist Church. About fifteen hundred people were present. King spent considerable time explaining the reasons why MIA leaders decided to recommend that we file a lawsuit in the federal court to overturn segregation laws that accounted for the bus protest. The people at the mass meeting approved the recommendation authorizing the MIA to file the proposed lawsuit in federal court.

About 9:15 p.m., while King was making an appeal for needed funds, his home was bombed. His wife, Coretta Scott King, and their daughter, and Mary Lucy, wife of Roscoe Williams, a close friend of the Kings, who were visiting them were not injured. A large crowd gathered at King's home. Like many others attending the mass meetings, I rushed to King's home. Most of the people who had gathered at King's home were angry and I felt that for the first time since the protest began that blacks would react violently. Standing on his porch and flanked by Sellers and Gayle, King joined with them in calling for calmness. The city commissioners promised a $500 reward for capture and conviction of the person responsible for the bombing. King's father, Martin Luther King, Sr., also known as Daddy King, phoned his son that night and early the next morning he and his other son, A.D., arrived in Montgomery after driving from Atlanta. Reportedly, he pleaded with his son, King Jr., urging him to leave Montgomery and move to Atlanta. King Jr. told him that he felt compelled to remain in Montgomery and continue to be involved in the protest.

On the last day of the first month of the year King and four other leaders met with Alabama Governor James E. Folsom to express their lack of confidence in the Montgomery police's commitment to protect black people. Black people considered Folsom to be a moderate segregationist. He had a black chauffeur named Winston Craig, who lived on Rutland Street, the same street that I lived on, in Mobile Heights. Although I cannot remember having actually ridden in the Governor's limousine, I did lean on it a few times while talking to Winston. He spent a considerable amount of time dusting and polishing that vehicle. Earlier Folsom had entertained Congressman Adam Clayton Powell, to the dismay of many whites in Alabama. Folsom was as much a liberal as any Southern politician in America. King told the governor that he wanted protection. Folsom said he would have state law enforcement officers keep an eye on King's home and that he would talk to the Montgomery County Sheriff. King also asked him about a permit to carry a gun in his car. The Governor said he would discuss that with the sheriff, too.

On February 1, the MIA executive board met to discuss the next step that we should take in the face of increased violence. The white violence against blacks had escalated, apparently urged on by the city officials' get-tough pronouncements. Some board members felt that we should begin to take direct action to protect ourselves, that some of us should get gun permits. It was agreed upon by members of the board that King, Abernathy and Hubbard be the first persons to apply for gun permits and, if they were successful, then others could apply for permits. We knew that we had a right to get gun permits but we also realized that rights for blacks were not considered by whites to be rights that they should respect. Although I did not have a permit to carry a gun, I kept a rifle and pistol in my home in the ready to fire position.

Attorneys Fred Gray and Charles Langford filed papers in federal court that same day. The suit sought an injunction against segregation on buses and also a halt to the harassment of the car pool. This meant that the "separate but equal," as it was labeled in the infamous 1896 "Plessy v. Ferguson" Supreme Court decision, had ceased to be a law that blacks in Montgomery were willing to accept any longer. By filing the suit in federal court we declared that black bus riders wanted to be treated the same as white bus riders. At the sheriff's office, King, Abernathy and Hubbard applied for a permits to allow them to carry a gun and to be night watchmen to protect King's home. Sheriff Mack Sim Bulter denied them permits. That same night a bomb exploded in Nixon's yard. Upon receiving word of the explosion a number of people assembled at his home. Again some of us felt that we should have and, if necessary, use weapons to protect ourselves. I suppose no one among us black leaders had a stronger desire to carry a gun to protect King and ourselves than Abernathy and myself. We both had served in the military. But Nixon, although not a veteran, was committed to pro-gun carrying to protect ourselves. More than anyone else, he was responsible for persuading King to ask Governor Folsom to help him secure a gun permit and to apply for one at the sheriff's department.

The city threatened to revoke Lewis' Citizens Club license if he continued to allow the MIA to use that premise for its headquarters. Once we became aware of that threat we immediately relocated temporarily back to the Negro Baptist Center, in the hope that we would soon find another place. But shortly after we returned to the Baptist Center the white Baptists had a meeting with the black trustees of the Baptist Center and expressed their objection to the MIA using the facility. Rev. Glasco, director of the Baptist Center, stated it this way during an executive board meeting: "There was a meeting held yesterday concerning the MIA using the Baptist Center for its headquarters. Dr. Davison, Superintendent of Missions for the white Baptist Association said that since the MIA is political it should seek another place." Continuing he said, "In the past any decision made concerning the Center's operation was made by the black trustees and the whites just went along with it, but they were adamant about the MIA ceasing to use the Baptist Center." The white Baptists contributed financially to the operation of the Baptist Center and black leaders did not want to jeopardize the work of the Center. The executive board agreed to move the headquarters to First Baptist Church. A few weeks later Nixon was instrumental in finding permanent space for the MIA headquarters in a building owned by the all-black Bricklayers Union.

It was reported to board members that Jeanetta Reese had withdrawn from the federal suit that had been filed by Gray, explaining that she and her husband had been threatened with economic retaliation and violence. Someone suggested that she had as great a need for protection as King. The other plaintiffs in the case

86

were Aurelia S. Browder, Susie McDonald, Claudette Colvin and Mary Louise Smith. The case was known as "Aurelia S. Browder v. William A. Gayle." Rosa Parks did not agree to be a plaintiff in the case even though one might think that she would have been first in line. But her conviction case that was on appeal may have had something to do with her not being a party in the federal case.

Four days later, white students rioted at the University of Alabama against the court-ordered admission of Autherine Lucy, the first black student to attend the school. The University's board of trustees responded by barring Lucy from attending classes. The local Selective Service Board changed Gray's draft classification from 4-D, an exempt status, to 1-A. Gray had been classified 4-D based on the fact that he was ordained as a minister by the Holt Street Church of Christ while he was still a teenager. However, after completing college at Alabama State College, he went to law school at Case Western Reserve University in Ohio and became a practicing attorney in Montgomery shortly before the bus boycott began. He maintained that he was both a lawyer and a minister.

That night we held a mass meeting at the Day Street Baptist Church where King told the audience that it was now clear that negotiations would not bring an end to the protest and that only a federal suit could enable us to achieve our objective of justice in bus transportation in Montgomery. He stated that the litigation might take a long time and that there was some uncertainty as to whether or not we should end the boycott. But he reaffirmed that the boycott is still on and that it may not end soon.

On February 8, two representatives of the Men of Montgomery, a white businessmen's group, said in an article that appeared in the *Montgomery Advertiser*, under the caption, "Group to Study Possibility of Ending Boycott of Buses," that the MIA executive board would consider ending the boycott. King said that any recommendations agreed upon by the board would be voted upon by a full meeting of the MIA at the next mass meeting. These two representatives, Joe Bear and C. J. Fitzpatrick, held discussions with the city officials over a five day period. Their plan called for the ten seats to be reserved for whites. They were not for anyone standing over a vacant seat. The Men of Montgomery also released a statement calling for an end to racial tension. Members of the MIA executive board were not impressed by their offer and as a consequence they did not consider it as a viable option. The following day in a telegram to President Eisenhower, AFL-CIO president George Meany urged an FBI investigation of violence in Montgomery and elsewhere in Alabama. At the mass meeting held at Bethel Baptist Church, Rev. Abernathy presided in the absence of King who had left for Chicago. Referring to the Men of Montgomery's offer to reach an agreement with the MIA to end the boycott Abernathy said, "It is too little too late."

On February 10, the Mississippi and Alabama White Citizens Councils drew eleven thousand people to the Montgomery Coliseum, in a gathering described as the largest segregation rally of the century. They cheered Mayor Gayle and Police Commissioner Sellers for their support of segregation on buses. Three days later, while King was still in Chicago preaching and meeting with leaders who were interested in the boycott, Judge Eugene Carter directed the Montgomery County Grand Jury to determine whether or not the boycott of Montgomery buses violated Alabama's anti-boycott law. In addition to having had two city detectives looking into MIA's early activities, Solicitor Thetford had summoned several MIA members, namely, Rufus Lewis, Rev. Wilson and MIA financial secretary, Erna A. Dungee, and bus manager, Bagley, to appear before the Gand Jury in his attempt to support his case. He also had the mayor testify.

On Thursday, February 16, King returned to Montgomery and addressed the MIA mass meeting at the First Baptist Church. The news was out that indictments of MIA leaders would soon be issued, charging them with engaging in an illegal boycott of buses. At that time, most of the leaders felt that these indictments would be against King and perhaps three or four other high-profile MIA leaders. We were not shocked because we realized that white people used the law and the courts to commit any travesty of justice they wanted to when it meant injustice against black folk.

Gray was charged by the Montgomery Grand Jury with "unlawful appearance as an attorney" for representing Reese after she had withdrawn from the suit. Gray had been indicted on trumped-up charges; nevertheless, it was of grave concern to MIA leaders since he was our lead attorney. On Monday February 20, the bus company and the city commission endorsed a proposal submitted to them by the Men of Montgomery. That night, when the seating plan suggested by that organization was presented to 3,000 people attending the mass meeting, the proposal was voted down by a margin of 2,998 to 2. It was observed that Rev. L. Roy Bennett and his assistant minister voted to accept it. After the meeting Abernathy contacted the Men of Montgomery and thanked them for their effort and informed them that their proposal was unacceptable to the people he represented. Commenting on the action taken at the mass meeting J. E. Pierce stated, "The morale of the masses, once again, revived the morale of the leaders."

After eleven weeks of boycotting Montgomery buses it was now clear to us that our pursuit was for desegregation rather than segregation in any form or hue on Montgomery buses. While nothing had been resolved by the boycott and while black people had paid a high price for not riding the buses, a much greater price than that paid by white folk who had merely lost money and felt emotionally threatened by the rise of black power in their midst, the bus boycotters remained joyful and peaceful. And above anything else, they were determined to "keep on keeping on" without any desire to turn back.

On February 21, 1956 the Montgomery County Grand Jury issued 115 indictments (later reduced to 90) to leaders and other participants in the Montgomery Bus Boycott, charging them with violating Alabama's 1921 statute against conspiracies that interfered with the Montgomery City Lines, Inc., carrying on lawful business.

THE STATE OF ALABAMA
Montgomery, Alabama
Circuit Court of Montgomery County February Term, A.D. 1956

The Grand Jury of said County charge that, before the finding of this indictment, M. L. King, Junior, Roy Bennett, E. N. French and E. D. Nixon, each of those names is to the Grand Jury otherwise unknown, did, without a just cause or legal excuse for so doing, enter into a combination, conspiracy, agreement, arrangement, or understanding for the purpose of hindering, delaying or preventing Montgomery City Lines, Inc., a corporation, from carrying on a lawful business, to-wit: the operation of a public transportation system in the City of Montgomery, Alabama, against the peace and dignity of the State of Alabama.

William F. Thetford
Solicitor
Fifteenth Judicial Circuit of Alabama

No. 7399
The State   Presented in open Court by the Foreman
vs.   of the Grand Jury in the presence of 17
M. L. KING, JR., ET AL   other members of the Grand Jury, this
        for   21 day of February, A. D. 1956
Vio. Sec. 54, Title 14, 1940
Code of Ala.   J. R. M.
Witnesses: Clerk of the Circuit Court of
See attached list   Montgomery, County
No Prosecutor,   Filed this 21 day of
A TRUE BILL   February, 1956
A. H. Wells   J. R. M.
Foreman of Grand Jury
G. J. No. 200   Clerk of the Circuit Court of
                     Montgomery County

Early Wednesday, February 22, the day following the issuance of indictments to leaders of the Montgomery Bus Boycott, my telephone began ringing and members of my church and some other people, including several MIA leaders called me, wanting to know how they might help me. Some wanted to know if I needed help in making bond. I told them that I had not been indicted as far as I knew. They were surprised and I was more surprised than anyone. I called Nixon who told me that he had been indicted and was on his way to the County Courthouse to turn himself in at the sheriff's office. When I let him know that I had not been indicted he said, "Just give them time, you will get your subpoena, too." About noon I joined some of those at the jail who were being arrested, posting bonds and being released. I spoke to an officer in Sheriff Mack Sim Butler's office there at the jail and was told that my name was not on the list of indicted persons. I, the secretary of the organization, had not been indicted? I was pleased to not have been indicted, but I could not understand the reason for it. "Maybe it was an oversight," I said to myself. I felt that I would soon know the reason. Jokingly I said to some of the indicted leaders, "Somebody has to run this organization while you fellows are in jail." King had been out of the city, speaking in Nashville, when Abernathy called to let him know that 115 leaders and other participants in the boycott had been indicted, including King and himself. King told Abernathy that he would return to Montgomery as soon as he could get a flight out of Nashville and that he would be there the next morning. He said that he would have to stop in Atlanta and pick up Coretta and Yoki, who were with his parents.

When King arrived in Atlanta he was met by a group of friends who were concerned about his well-being. They had assembled at the request of Daddy King. Included were some of Atlanta's most distinguished citizens, including Benjamin E. Mays, president of Morehouse College. Daddy King endeavored to persuade King to remain in Atlanta. He did for a day, but Daddy King meant that he should not return to Montgomery. It appeared that people in that group of about nine favored Daddy King's advice to his son. Then King told him that he could not turn his back on his friends in Montgomery, regardless of the consequences. He said, "I would rather go back and spend time in jail than not to go back." After listening to King speak, Dr. Mays expressed the opinion that King was right in wanting to return to Montgomery. Then others in the group agreed that King needed to go back to Montgomery.

On Thursday, February 23, King, his father and family drove to Montgomery. Immediately after arriving in Montgomery, he went to the County jail where he was arrested, photographed with the number 7089 hanging under his chin and released on bond. He was the twenty-fourth person to be booked. King agreed to plead guilty to the speeding ticket he had received in January. Gray told him that on the day before, while many of the other indicted leaders were being arrested, Judge Carter upheld the conviction of Parks by the recorder's court and that city attorneys moved to dismiss the suit that he and Langford had taken to the federal district court.

Abernathy and I informed King that members of the executive board had agreed that we should have a mass meeting at First Baptist Church that night and that Friday had been designated as Montgomery's Prayer and Pilgrimage Day, "carless" day when all supporters of the protest would walk. This was also the day when the indicted leaders would be arraigned in the circuit court on boycott-related charges.

The more immediate concern for us that afternoon was the

meeting MIA leaders had with Arthur D. Shores and his assistant
Peter Hall, both Birmingham attorneys who had been sent to
Montgomery by the NAACP. Attorney Shores agreed to represent all
ninety people at a fee of $100 per person, but no more than $9,000.
Funds were coming to the MIA, but car pool expenses were in excess
of $3,000 a week. We still were not sure where this money would
come from, but we were pleased that we had competent attorneys to
represent us. Roy Wilkins had talked by telephone with King while
he was in Atlanta and promised that the NAACP would assist in the
legal defense and that afternoon he sent this telegram to King:

*All our people over the nation and millions of friends stand with
you and your courageous fellow citizens as you answer the
indictment of the grand jury. We will continue to offer legal advice
upon your request. Please do not hesitate to call on us.*

People began to gather in the afternoon for the 7:00 p.m. rally.
Over four thousand people were present to hear King speak and to
get additional information on the indictments and to learn how they
would effect the boycott. After much singing and praising God the
program began. King spoke of the injustices and suffering that we
had endured and how we decided to use protest to defeat injustice.
He said, "If we are arrested every day, if we are exploited every day,
if we are trampled over every day, don't ever let anyone pull you so
low as to cause you to hate him." He added, "Love is our only
weapon."

This was the first time that so much national attention had been
given to Montgomery since the protest began. There were more than
thirty-five reporters present, including an ABC commentator. Major
newspapers, including *The New York Times*, that had carried front-
page accounts about the indictments. Other race activist groups in
addition to the NAACP were present and some activists, including
Bayard Rustin, an ally of A. Phillip Randolph, wanted to help. Some
people donated money and others pledged their financial support to
the Montgomery movement. It was announced that the next mass
meeting would be held Monday at the Holt Street Baptist Church.
The next day indicted leaders were arraigned in the circuit court and
pleaded not guilty to boycott-related charges. Judge Carter assigned

a trial date for the week of March 19. This was the day of the pilgrimage when many bus boycotters and supporters of the boycott were praying and walking. That evening, a group of MIA leaders met with Rustin and listened to him echo King's message of nonviolence. I was not impressed with his message, but I recognized that he was a true believer of what he proclaimed and that had a positive impact upon me. Few things can cause me to rise up and express my wrath or indignation as hypocrisy. Conversely, honesty, especially when it is coupled with steadfastness, touches me in such a way that I am usually compelled to respond with compassion.

On Monday, February 27, the MIA held an executive board meeting. Various comments were made on the indictments of leaders and the orderly manner in which those indicted had responded. Again, some people expressed surprise that I had not been indicted, and again I said, jokingly, "Since you people are going to be in jail somebody has to carry on the protest." We were concerned about the trial that would begin on March 19, and how we may be more effective in raising money to pay our leal expenses. King said the NAACP had promised to assist us in our legal expenses, i.e., paying a part of the lawyers' fees for Arthur Shores and Peter Hall. Also discussed was the cost for operating the car pool, the need for paid staff and office workers. King stated that some money had come in since the indictments. He said that William H. Gray, pastor of Bright Hope Baptist Church in Philadelphia had called him earlier that day and said that the Baptist Ministers Conference of Philadelphia had put $1,500 in the mail for the MIA. Other ministerial groups had pledged thirty thousand dollars that would be payable by the date of the trial. While we leaders in Montgomery were hopeful, it was still too early to tell how much financial support the MIA would receive. However, we were gratified by the response people outside of Montgomery were making. Since the indictments, $5,000 had already been received and that amounted to about a third of the amount of money the MIA had received prior to the indictments. Members of the board were more concerned than even before about depositing MIA's money in banks in Montgomery. Realizing that any thing anti-boycott white folk asked judges to do was granted, the board authorized president King, treasurer Nixon and Financial secretary Erna Dungee to deposit money donated to the MIA in banks in Georgia, New York and Oklahoma to begin with, and banks in other states may be used in the future should it become necessary in order to prevent Alabama judges from freezing MIA assets.

Some board members expressed their feelings about Rev. Bennett, who, with his assistant minister, had voted for the compromise seating proposal mediated by the Men of Montgomery on February 20 that other mass meeting attendees voted against. Bennett spoke in his own defense, noting that the MIA began in Mt. Zion AMEZ Church where he was the pastor. He also said that his congregation had suffered as much as any congregation in Montgomery as a result of the boycott. Then he said, "I accept, the majority wins." King said that Bennett had a right to dissent and encouraged the leaders to remain united and prepare for the trials." He also said that people from across America had written to encourage us. He called the names of some distinguished Americans who had sent letters and telegrams. Later that evening a mass meeting was held at the Holt Street Baptist Church. Some people gathered to pray two hours before the 7:00 p.m. meeting. When I arrived at the church at 6:30 p.m., the church was filled and overflowing. The huge crowd reminded me of the first mass meeting that had been held at that same church.

King presided over the meeting. After greeting everyone, he asked Lewis, chairman of the transportation committee, to come to the lectern. Lewis expressed concern that the mass arrest may have an adverse effect on the car pool. He urged more people to use their cars, to become drivers and dispatchers and to pick-up their neighbors who needed rides. Abernathy said that arresting leaders would not stop this movement because it was the people's movement and the people are determined to continue the boycott until justice runs down like a mighty stream.

King said that with the arrest of nearly a hundred of our leaders this protest movement had reached beyond Montgomery and got the attention of people across America and in some other nations of the world. He emphasized that we should turn the other check and use Christian principles, love and passive resistance rather than the methods of violence and hate that are being used by the White Citizens Council and other hate groups in Montgomery. Responding to what some people were saying about Bennett, King said, "Rev.

[handwritten: arrests to end the movement, but opposite effect with national recognition + press cov]

Bennett, our dear brother, who has devoted so much to this movement, voted to stop the protest because he felt that was the right thing to do. He exercised his democratic right to vote the way he did. We should respect him for his courage, even though most of us did not vote the same way as he did." He then asked the people to cease calling Mrs. Reese who had withdrawn her name as a plaintiff in the federal lawsuit. We must allow love to direct us in all our endeavors.

On Tuesday, February 28, Glenn E. Smiley, field secretary of the Fellowship of Reconciliation (FOR), based in New York, arrived in Montgomery. He had the blessings of A. Philip Randolph and Charles R. Lawrence, II, national chair of FOR who had written King on February 24 with an offer to help the MIA. He told King that Reverend Glenn F. Smiley would be coming to Montgomery early next week as a representative of FOR. King had also heard about Smiley from Rustin. Smiley interviewed King shortly after they met. With an armful of books he talked with King about nonviolence and the Gandhian approach to confronting oppressors. King was pleased with what he heard.

On March 1, I received three subpoenas that directed me, secretary of the MIA, to appear as a witness for the State of Alabama and testify against Reverend M. L. King, Jr., Reverend W. J. Powell and Mose Bishop. "Duces Tecum," summons instructed me "to bring and produce all minutes of meetings of the Montgomery Improvement Association." Rev. Powell was the pastor of the Old Ship AMEZ Church and a member of the MIA executive board. Mose Bishop, also known as M. Pleasure, Jr., for a brief period of time, served as the MIA executive secretary and administrative assistant to King. He had served as alumni secretary at Dillard University. He didn't get along with some of the MIA leaders, however, at the time of the indictments, he was involved with the inner workings of the MIA. I recall that he resisted giving me information on some financial transactions that I had requested. It was only after he was confronted by Nixon that he turned over some receipts that I wanted for my records.

It was not until I received these subpoenas that I realized why I had not been indicted. I was to be the star witness for the State of Alabama. Immediately, after receiving these summons, I called King and told him that I had received three subpoenas and one of them

95

was to testify against him in the March 19 trial. I also informed him that I had been ordered to bring the MIA minutes of all meetings. King said, "They got you after all. I wondered why they had not indicted you. Now we know why." King and I agreed to talk later and discuss the implications and ramifications of my being asked to submit MIA minutes at the trial. Then I called Charles Langford, my personal attorney. I wanted to know from him whether or not I had to produce all the minutes of MIA meetings. After reading what the summons said, Langford advised me to bring all the minutes to the trial. Subsequently, King, Gray, Langford and I reviewed the minutes. There were some things in the minutes that we would rather not have to present at the trial, but we felt that the prosecutors would use any information we presented to help the State to get a guilty verdict and we did not think that we had anything to hide. We all agreed with Langford that I should submit all my minutes to the trial.

Gray filed a bill of demurrer in Montgomery Circuit Court charging that the 1921 Alabama anti-boycott law used to arrest the bus boycott leaders was unconstitutional. On Monday, March 1, the second mass meeting following the indictment of ninety-plus leaders was held at the Hutchinson Street Baptist Church. After nearly two hours of praying, singing and testifying, the mass meeting began at 7:00 p.m. Rev. B. D. Lambert, pastor of the Maggie Street Baptist Church, offered prayer. His prayer was more of a sermonette than a prayer. It certainly was not modeled after Jesus's sentence prayers. I read one of my favorite passages of Scriptures, the entire thirteenth chapter of First Corinthians, that is sometimes referred to as the "love chapter" of the Bible. After we sang "What a Friend We have in Jesus," King greeted the people and said, "We have among us a number of distinguished guests. I must decrease that they may increase. God is using Montgomery as a proving ground." Then he presented guests who were asked to give brief remarks. Among them were Owen D. Pelt, pastor of Shiloh Baptist Church in Chicago where King had preached that church's anniversary sermon two weeks earlier; A. Sanders, representative for the United Auto Workers in Chicago, Thomas Kilgore, Jr. pastor of Friendship Baptist Church in New York; a representative for ministers of Cleveland whose name I do not recall; Sandy F. Ray, pastor of Cornerstone Baptist Church in Brooklyn; Glen E. Smiley, national field secretary for the Fellowship of Reconciliation, and M. L. King, Sr., who was the last of the guests to speak. He got the loudest applause when he said, "I am no outsider: I have vested interest here, and if things get too hot I shall move in." This was the same Daddy King who wanted his son to remain in Atlanta and not face the music of the indictments just a little more than a week earlier. Smiley was the only white person to speak. It was a bit unusual for a white person to speak at a mass meeting since Rev. Robert Graetz was usually the only white person who attended the meetings, except for white news reporters. Smiley was well received. He wrote his wife a letter that night and said, "When I made my first point, the house almost came apart. You see, there are so few, if any, white ministers who will come out and speak at all." I think it was more than just a white person being present that won the people. Other blacks in that audience, like myself, could recognize that Smiley was authentic and desired freedom and justice for all.

More than $12,000 was raised that night to help the MIA pay for the trials and, to be sure, that was the highlight of the meeting. This was a huge morale booster for the MIA leaders who, at that time, could only see that nearly a hundred bus boycott activists had to stand trial. The next two weeks focused on leaders of the boycott preparing themselves emotionally and spiritually for the trial. A lot of support, letters, telegrams and money were being received. Some people informed the MIA that they would be coming to Montgomery for the trials. On March 5, a mass meeting was held at the Bethel Baptist Church, where Reverend Hubbard was the pastor. During that meeting Hubbard suggested that all persons who had been indicted should dress-up for the trial. As he put it, "Wear your Sunday best." He emphasized that we were not criminals. "We are the sons and daughters of God," he declared. The next day Alabama State legislators introduced strict new racial segregation bills in the legislature. One of them was aimed at strengthening by law segregation on buses and at public events. It had the ring of apartheid. On Thursday, Gray and Langford amended "Browder v. Gayle," removing Reese from the list of plaintiffs.

On Monday, March 12, the MIA executive board held its last meeting before the trial. During that meeting King talked about the legal staff, noting that everything seems to be in place. He said that the legal team would consist of our own attorneys, Gray and Langford, NAACP lawyers Arthur D. Shores, Orzell Billingsley, Jr., Peter Hall and NAACP general counsel, Robert L. Carter. We were much encouraged by the response of people from across America to our ordeal in Montgomery. Nixon reported $2,000 that he said had been dropped in the mail slot of the front door of his home. That same day ninety-six United States Congressmen from eleven southern states issued a "Southern Manifesto," which declared the "Brown v. Board of Education" decision an abuse of judicial power and pledged to use all lawful means to resist its implementation. The following day Governor Folsom publicly denounced "mobocracy" and urged Montgomery city officials and black leaders to reach a settlement of the bus boycott.

Based on FBI Director J. Edgar Hoover's briefing, made at the request of President Eisenhower, five days before he said at a March 14 weekly news conference that he wanted a congressional joint commission established to facilitate a meeting of black and white leaders from the South, he had refused to act on Attorney General Herbert Brownell's proposal that called for the creation of an independent Civil Rights Commission to gather facts about voting rights violations and economic reprisals against Negroes.

On Sunday, the eve of the trial against boycott leaders, King preached at Dexter Avenue Baptist Church on the subject, "When Peace Becomes Obnoxious." On that same day, although I had been summoned to appear in court the following day at the beginning of the trial, I spoke at a NAACP-sponsored rally at the Soldiers and Sailors Memorial Hall in Pittsburgh. I was introduced to that enthusiastic audience by AMEZ Church Bishop Charles H. Foggie. Nearly $3,000 was raised for the MIA during that event. Earlier that day I had preached on the subject, "Love is What Love Does" at the Macedonia Baptist Church, pastored by the Rev. T. P. Twiggs. That church gave me a $235 honorarium. After speaking at the afternoon rally I boarded an airplane and returned to Montgomery, arriving in time to answer the next day the summons that I had received.

The names of two outsiders who have already been briefly mentioned deserve a more elaborate look. I refer to Bayard Rustin and Glenn F. Smiley. There were not any other outsiders who had as much impact on the Montgomery protest as either of these men. They impacted King more than any other two persons. Only Abernathy who was an insider, King's companion, impacted him as much as either of these two men.

Bayard Rustin was a colorful character. After a stint as an organizer with the young Communists League, he joined the Fellowship for Reconciliation where he served as a field secretary and then as a race relations director. He was a close associate of A. Philip Randolph and a devout Quaker. Rustin was sentenced to twenty-eight months in prison in 1942 as a conscientious objector to World War II. He directed the Free India Company and led sit-ins at the British Embassy in Washington in 1955. A founder of the Congress of Racial Equality (CORE), he conducted the organization's first Freedom Ride through the South in 1947. In 1953 he resigned from FOR and joined the staff of War Resisters League, as its executive secretary.

Rustin, a longtime advocate of nonviolence, arrived in Montgomery from New York on February 21, the same day the Montgomery grand jury indicted 115 boycott leaders. His primary objective was to talk with King, who at the time was participating in the Religious Emphasis Week at Fisk University in Nashville. The next morning following his arrival in Montgomery, Rustin knocked on Abernathy's door with references he was carrying with him, including one from A. Philip Randolph, who had supported the boycott as well as paid for Rustin's trip to Montgomery. That was a day Abernathy was not in a mood to spend time with a stranger. So he begged off any long discussion about the boycott. Later that day Rustin talked with Nixon, who had a much lengthier conversation with him. Like Rustin, Nixon also admired A. Philip Randolph. As a matter of fact, Nixon had years before organized a chapter of Randolph's Brotherhood of Sleeping Car Porters in Montgomery.

That same day, boycott leaders were being arrested and posting bonds. Rustin, although staying in the background, persuaded a friend to write him a loan of $5,000 that he turned over to Nixon to help make bond for those who needed it. It had been Rustin, earlier in the day, who had suggested to Nixon that he go into the courthouse and turn himself in before the deputies came for him. Nixon had done just that and became the first of those indicted persons to be arrested and released on bond. At the end of the day Rustin went to the home of Jeanetta Reese, the woman who had withdrawn from the federal lawsuit. There were two police cars in front of Reese's home. Rustin told the two policemen that he was a journalist working for *Le Figaro* and *Manchester Guardian*. One of the policemen wrote that down, as Rustin explained to them something of the importance of the French and British publications. He didn't get much from his conversation with Mrs. Reese. It was obvious to him that she was a frightened woman. She told him, "I had to do what I did or I probably wouldn't be alive today."

The next day King arrived in Montgomery and was briefed on the indictments by Abernathy. After he was arrested and released on bond, on the recommendation of Nixon and in the presence of Abernathy and myself, he invited Rustin to a meeting of the strategy committee which was also a meeting where seven persons offered prayers. They all emphasized peace, nonviolence and justice. Rustin was inspired by what he saw and heard. Later he informed FOR's John Swomley, executive director of the organization, that King was using the Gandhian approach of passive resistance. Rustin was concerned as to whether he, an outsider, could work in the interest of the protest, but he offered his help and decided to be involved in the protest. For it was a cause which he had lived to be a part of, as attested to by his colorful and sometimes daring life. King told him that the people in Montgomery could use all the help they could get and stressed the fact that we, as a people, are in this struggle together for justice whether we live in the South or in the North and whether we are black or white. Rustin gave one of his Quaker "Amens" to that as it was expressed in silence accompanied by a stare-like look that said it all.

That night Rustin came to the mass meeting held at Abernathy's First Baptist Church. There were thirty or forty others there, but none of them knew of the man from *Le Figaro*, but some had seen him as an ostentatious character in Greenwich Village. Some of these reporters spoke to a reporter from the *Montgomery Advertiser* about this man with the foreign papers. This local reporter got in touch with the local police, as suspicion arose about his identity. Some reporters even talked about calling Paris and London to find out who was this man representing the *Le Figaro* and *Manchester Guardian* publications.

Rustin called John Swomley in New York and told him about the protest and what he had experienced, but most of all he talked with him about the need for these people in Montgomery to have someone to come and teach them nonviolence. He said that he would not be staying in Montgomery. The word was out that Rustin was an imposter and even worse, if the white people found out about him they would use the information to discredit everything the boycott had accomplished. A black reporter from the *Birmingham World* got word that Rustin was in Montgomery. Knowing about his background he insisted that Rustin leave town. That evening Rustin met with King. On Saturday, February 25, a group of the MIA strategists met to discuss whether or not Rustin should be allowed to stay in Montgomery. Rev. A. W. Wilson had already told news reporters, without having mentioned Rustin, that the protest was a local matter and not for outside agitators. Nixon and King were for Rustin remaining in Montgomery, and Abernathy, somewhat reluctantly, sided with them. I was not sure, but tended to agree with Rev. Wilson, in the case of Rustin. And I say, in the case of Rustin, because, as a rule, I did not accept black people allowing white people to determine who their leaders or friends should be. But it was Rustin's former Communist Party involvement that concerned me most. I recalled how Paul Robeson was discredited by the U. S. Government and subjected to many kinds of pressures and violent treatment because he associated with Communists. Even some Negroes avoided Robeson after the government discredited him. On Sunday, Rustin attended the Dexter Avenue Baptist Church and heard King preach on "Faith in Man." Later that evening he met with King at his parsonage where they chatted about nonviolence and what King called "passive resistance." King was impressed with Rustin's knowledge of and devotion to nonviolence.

On Monday, February 27, the word circulated that Rustin might be arrested or charged with committing fraud, or even worse, be exposed in the newspapers as being all those things that he had been labeled as being, including a bastard, a Negro, an ex-Communist, conscientious objector, ex-con and a homosexual. A black newspaper reporter in Birmingham clinched things when he threatened to expose Rustin in the next issue of his newspaper unless MIA leaders got him out of town, immediately. Rustin didn't want to leave, but he certainly didn't want to, in any way whatsoever, damage himself or the protest movement. He was visibly hurt by what was now apparent to him, that he would have to leave Montgomery. We boycott leaders agreed to ask Rustin to leave Montgomery. That evening Nixon, who was hurt more than any of the other leaders, called Randolph in New York to find out more about Rustin, who had worked for him. Randolph defended his assistant, but expressed to some of his colleagues the concerns Montgomerians had about him being there. On Tuesday, Randolph convened a group of some twenty-odd people to consider the matter of Rustin and his presence in Montgomery. After that meeting, Swomley immediately informed Smiley, who had just arrived in Montgomery to replace Rustin. He wanted him to know that a group of New York leaders, including himself, had met and determined that Rustin could make for trouble in Montgomery. Smiley was ordered to keep away from Rustin, to not be seen with him. Rustin, partially in disguise, was smuggled to Birmingham in the back of an automobile. But this would not be the end of Rustin's impact on the Montgomery protest movement. Like "truth crushed to earth" he, too, was destined to "rise again."

The other outsider was Glenn F. Smiley, a white field secretary of FOR. Swomley and Charles Lawrence had agreed that Rustin should not be in Montgomery, and they both were in agreement that Smiley should be there. They felt that he would be of valuable service to the movement. Shortly after arriving in Montgomery, Smiley, a mild-mannered minister with a somewhat unassuming demeanor from Texas who, like Rustin, was imprisoned for pacifist resistance during World War II, met with King for the purpose of having an interview with him. During that meeting he talked with King about nonviolence and told him that he was a believer in the Gandhian method of nonviolence. He let him see some of the books he had brought with him that had helped him in understanding nonviolence. He wanted to know about King's knowledge of nonviolence. King admitted that he knew a few quality quotes by Gandhi, but that he knew very little about the man. Then he said he knew much more about Henry David Thoreau and his civil disobedience approach to confronting injustice. Continuing he said, "It seems that Gandhi and Thoreau had a lot in common. I admire them both." Smiley remarked that Gandhi, using nonviolence, was able to stand against overwhelming odds and gain freedom for the people of India. He described Gandhi's philosophy, in essence, as not retaliating against evil. The refusal to do so was based on a realization that "the law of retaliation is the law of the multiplication of evil." King told Smiley that he was quite impressed by the things he had heard and said, "we will have to talk more soon."

Initially, some MIA leaders were skeptical about Smiley suddenly arriving on the scene following the Rustin affair, and besides that, he was white. Some black leaders felt that he might be working with the local police or F.B.I. Director J. Edgar Hoover. Admittedly, I was somewhat skeptical of his involvement. But Smiley was enjoying himself as he began familiarizing himself with the Montgomery protest, its objectives and leaders. Upon meeting Smiley face-to-face, I was not impressed, and upon learning that he was from Texas rather than New York, as I had thought, only hardened my feelings about him. My feeling about Southern white men was at least a notch below my feelings about Northern white men. I also had strong feelings about the wisdom of anyone teaching black people who are the victims of white violence to be nonviolent. I had heard enough of that kind of preaching from King and I did not relish the thought of a white man coming to Montgomery to tell us more about the importance of being nonviolent. I even said to some black leaders, "If Smiley wanted to talk about being nonviolent he should talk to white people because they, not us, are the violent people in Montgomery." But I would soon discover that Smiley was authentic and that he had a deep and sincere conviction about the philosophy of nonviolence that he advocated. I reasoned that he and Rev. Graetz were of the same spirit.

Smiley and Rustin, two outsiders, would contribute generously and admirably to the Montgomery movement. Smiley would be the first white man to ride on an integrated bus in Montgomery as he sat with King early on that first day blacks returned to riding the buses after having boycotted them for over a year. Rustin, who had continued to support the protest while still in Birmingham and New York where he was when word came that the buses in Montgomery were integrated, returned to Montgomery in time to rejoice in knowing that integration had come to the buses in Montgomery. He had also arrived just in time to inspect the damage from a shotgun blast fired into King's home early that Sunday morning on December 23 by die-hard racists who remained determined that there would not be desegregation on Montgomery buses. But they would not be able by their violence to prevent what nonviolence had played a role in achieving. Rustin and Smiley had played a significant part in the revolution of love that transformed Montgomery. Without these two outsiders, the protest may have become violent. I could have been one of those persons who struck the blow that would have started a violent revolution in Montgomery. But these men convinced me and some other militant blacks that it was probably best, after all, for us to pursue nonviolence. To say that they contributed significantly to the protest does not, in any way whatsoever, take anything away from King, Abernathy, Nixon, and other leaders who in solidarity walked into battle and refused to fire a shot even while being shot at. Like the Hebrew Boys who were thrown into the fiery furnace, these leaders did not cease to delight in the Presence of their Deliverer. I feel that King would not have been able to expand his knowledge of nonviolence as he did had it not been for his relationship with Smiley and Rustin, who, themselves, were no less than he committed to the destruction of bus segregation in Montgomery. Remember, before King met these two men, he had been persuaded to, and did apply for, a permit to carry a gun. Without his interaction with Smiley and Rustin I feel that King would have not been able to prevent blacks from retaliating, in kind, toward those whites who violently attacked blacks. But this did not happen and I feel that this was attributed to the impact Rustin and Smiley had on King. Before discussing the actualization of the desegregation of buses in Montgomery there were many other events and developments that occurred during the next two-thirds of the life span of the Montgomery Bus Boycott. Let us now turn to the four-day trial of Martin Luther King, Jr.

Alabama Solicitor William F. Thetford and the defense lawyers reached an agreement before the trial began to put on trial MIA president, Martin Luther King, Jr., as the first of the ninety indicted defendants to be tried. His trial would be a test case. The four-day trial began Monday, March 19. There were great expectations, curiosity and a sense of wonderment in the courtroom. Some thirty-odd reporters had come for the trial. About a fourth of them were black reporters. There were national and foreign reporters. The *New York Times* that had already given front-page coverage to the indictments was present for the trial. Journalists from more than ten foreign nations that included Japan, Germany and Australia were present. Reporters had come from India and France and Alastair Cooke of the *Manchester Guardian*, the publication that almost landed Rustin in prison or the protest in a tumultuous discreditness was also present.

Now it was that unpropitious time for the trial to begin. Eighty-nine of the indictments had been held in abeyance as the State of Alabama pronounced King alone as an alleged criminal who prosecutors wanted to destroy more than they did any one or the rest of the indicted persons combined. I had already entered the courthouse that seated about 230 people. Nearly half of the seats were reserved for the defendants and for the approximately eighty witnesses. As ordered in the "Duces Tecum" summons I had received I brought with me all the minutes of the Montgomery Improvement Association that were in my care. Sitting in the courtroom I began to sing softly, mostly in a humming fashion, barely audible to myself, "Amazing Grace." As I was humming the words,

Twas grace that brought me safe this far
And grace will lead me on,

King entered the courtroom. He was accompanied by his wife, Coretta Scott, Daddy King, his mother, Alberta Williams, and out-of-state visitors that included Congressman Charles Diggs, Jr., of Michigan.

Then Judge Eugene Carter entered the courtroom as the bailiff announced that the court was now in session. The prosecution, led by Circuit Solicitor Thetford and his team of lawyers, would call twenty-seven witnesses in an attempt to prove that King was the primary leader of the boycott, responsible for formulating and executing plans, presiding at meetings, authorizing financial expenditures, and representing the MIA in negotiations. I would be a star witness for the State of Alabama. Some of the State's witnesses were people who were connected with the MIA and, of course, like myself, they did not want to testify against King. On the first day of the trial the prosecution set out to prove that the MIA had instigated and maintained the boycott without "just cause" or "legal excuse," the black violence had helped enforce the boycott and that King had led the MIA's effort—all in violation of the state anti-boycott statute. Among those called to the witness stand were Rev. A. W. Wilson, pastor of the Holt Street Baptist Church, the site where the first bus boycott mass meeting had been held. It seemed that he did not remember that King was at his church on the night the boycott began or what actually happened that night. Of course, that was not true. Rev. Robert S. Graetz, a white pastor of the Trinity Lutheran Church whose membership, except for members of his own family, were black, said that King had not asked people to boycott the buses, rather he urged them to decide for themselves. The MIA's financial secretary, Erna Dungee, was questioned about finances and she could not remember when the boycott had started, but had records to show that finances had been raised to support the boycott. Mayor Gayle testified that the MIA had negotiated with him over ending the protest which was evidence that they had conspired to boycott the buses.

That night two huge mass meetings were held at the St. John AMEZ Church and the Day Street Baptist Church. King told the people at both mass meetings that this would be the year when God would set his people free. He also said that he was not discouraged, but much to the contrary, greatly encouraged by the support we were receiving from people across America. He noted that this fight for justice is much bigger than Montgomery. Two MIA mass meetings were announced for Tuesday night, one at Bethel Baptist Church and the other one at the Beulah Baptist Church. Attendees were told that their continued presence at the courthouse during this trial was important even though most of them would not be able to enter the much too small courtroom. No one was able to predict how long the trial would last. There was speculation that it would last for at least a week, probably two weeks.

On the second day of the trial the prosecution sought to link the incidents of shootings on buses with the boycott leadership. At last, the state of Alabama's star witness was called to the stand. I, Uriah J. Fields, secretary of the MIA, was that state witness or, at least the

State had hoped that I would be. I had the minutes of MIA meetings, beginning with the minute of the organizing meeting of the MIA that occurred on December 5. That made me a very important witness. I had the record that the prosecution would use in an attempt to convict King and hopefully the rest of those indicted leaders. After I duly affirmed, rather than be sworn because I refused to swear to tell the truth, Solicitor Thetford asked me to give my name and occupation. Then I was questioned as to whether or not these minutes were, in fact, the minutes of MIA meetings that I had recorded. To that question I answered in the affirmative. The prosecutor read certain statements from the minutes and asked me whether or not they were in the minutes. Again I responded a number of times in the affirmative. At one point I was asked to describe what happened during a typical meeting. In my response to that question I said, "At one mass meeting the speaker was Rev. E. N. French, who talked about 'togethemess'. He illustrated 'togetherness' by taking a single banana from a bunch of about seven bananas he was holding in his hands and peeled it. While waving the peeled banana he said, 'This is what happens when you don't stick together; you get skint.'" Unlike some of my colleagues who testified, including Wilson and Graetz who, indeed, committed perjury or at least did not tell the truth that they knew, and King who later did not tell the whole truth, I found no need to speak anything other than the truth, and besides, what I had written was the record. My lying would not have changed the record. My tactic was to be reticent and in certain instances give the answers to questions not asked rather than to questions asked. I was chided several times by the prosecutor and Judge who ordered me to answer the questions. I felt that what I said would not be as important as what I had written; however, I had no intention of providing the court with any more information than I was required to give. After the trial, the *Montgomery Advertiser* reported that solicitor Thetford said that I was the most recalcitrant witness to have been summoned by the State during his more than a decade as solicitor.

The two Tuesday night mass meetings at Bethel Baptist Church and Beulah Baptist Church were well attended. Abernathy spoke at Bethel and Nixon spoke at Belulah. King attended both of these meetings which were held at churches on the opposite side of the city. There was some hope that we would win in the court, i.e., not be found guilty of conducting an illegal boycott. Nixon, however, was under no such illusion. He said, "If they found Rosa Parks guilty, surely they are going to find King guilty." He added, "All of us may end up in jail, but that is the price we may have to pay for justice."

On Wednesday, March 21, after making an unsuccessful motion to exclude the state's evidence, King's defense began its presentation. The team consisted of six lawyers: Fred Gray, Charles D. Langford, NAACP lawyers Arthur D. Shores, Orzel Billingsley, Jr., Peter Hall, and NAACP lawyer Robert L. Carter, who was unable to participate in the proceedings because he was not a member of the Alabama Bar. The defense endeavored to show that bus segregation was abusive and that Montgomery blacks had suffered for years from Montgomery bus drivers, thus establishing under the 1921 anti-boycott law a "just cause" or "legal excuse" for the boycott. Of the thirty-five defense witnesses, thirty-one of them were bus patrons who told of their experiences of abuse by bus drivers and the justification and motivation for their own decision to boycott the buses. Georgia Gilmore, for example, said that once a bus driver had told her, after she paid for her fare, "'Nigger, get out that door and go around to the back door.' He then sped away before I could reboard the bus." Most of the black witnesses testified that their decision to boycott the buses was spontaneous and that King did not tell them to boycott the buses.

On the final day of the trial, Thelma Glass, a member of the Women's Political Council, testified about her group's long and unsuccessful efforts to improve conditions on the buses, and others of the defense witnesses described the humiliations they had been subjected to on the buses. Then defense lawyer Arthur Shores called King to the stand. Having been duly sworn King was asked by Shores: "Are you one of the organizers of the Montgomery Improvement Association?" King responded, "Yes, I am." The lawyer wanted to know, "How does one become a member of the MIA, was there a joining fee or dues?" King said becoming a member is just a matter of being interested in improving Montgomery and there were no dues or membership fee. Some of the other questions taken verbatim from the transcript of the trial are as follows:

Q: From what source is the Association receiving funds?

A: Well, the funds have been received from free-will offerings, individuals who have given freely for the fund. ...

Q: Are members of the Montgomery Improvement Association restricted by race or to any particular race?

A: No, not at all, anyone. ...

Q: During the course of your speeches have you urged any of the listeners or members of the MIA to refrain from riding the buses of Montgomery City Lines?

A: No, I have not. My exposition has always been "to let your conscience be your guide, if you want to ride, that is all right."

Q: Have those meetings always been open to anybody, the members, as well as all citizens?

A: Yes, they have. ...

Q: Will you describe the operation of the car pool?

A: Well, the car pool is just a matter of individuals volunteering to give their cars for the purpose of transporting persons to and from their jobs and their businesses. These persons volunteered to place their cars in the pool from the pick-up stations and dispatch stations, and these cars will be there at certain hours for the purpose of transporting people to various places.

Q: Are the persons charged any fee for being transported?

A: No, they are not.

Q: Are the persons paid for operating their cars?

A: No.

Q: Is there any payment made to persons who own cars?

A: No.

Q: To operate them in the Pool? Or anything?

A: Well, there is a payment which is for the purpose of upkeep—that is for the wear and tear on the cars. We have all day drivers, about twenty all day drivers that start at six o'clock in the morning and work throughout the day, and there is a bonus given for the purpose of wear and tear on the car, and no one is paid a salary for driving.

Q: Are you paid a salary by the Montgomery Improvement Association?

A: No, I am not.

Q: I believe some statement was made about a telephone conversation between you and the Mayor where terms of the proposal were accepted by you and later rejected. Did you receive any proposal from the Mayor with respect to the settlement of the controversy over the telephone? And later reject it?

A: No, I did not. I have never received a proposal that I accepted. I have always contended I could only take it up with the people, and that is what I said to Mayor Gayle, when he offered the proposal over the phone, I would take it up with the people, and that is as far as I would go. And he was to call me back on Friday to discuss it, but he never called back.

Q: And have you always taken the proposals to the people to have them decide whether or not the proposal would be accepted?

A: Yes, sir, I have.

Q: And what has been the result of taking the proposals back to the people?

A: Well, to this point all of the proposals I took to the people and put before them they felt were not satisfactory so they have rejected the proposals to this point.

Q: Have you any concern for the status of Negroes in Montgomery?

THE SOLICITOR: We object to that.

THE COURT: If you connect it up with the Montgomery Improvement Association as a member.

BY LAWYER SHORES:

Q: Does everyone connect it with the Montgomery Improvement Association?

A: Yes, they do have concern for the general status of Negroes here.

Q: Is it, or not, a fact your activities in connection with the Montgomery Improvement Association constitute a part of your effort to improve the Negro status in Montgomery?

A: That is right, quite right.

Q: In connection with the transportation?

A: Yes.

Q: Do you recall what amount was paid?

A: No, I don't remember the exact amount off hand.

Q: The finances are not handled by you, are they?

A: No.

Q: You have a finance committee?

A: That is right.

Q: Is there an office worker that receives any pay?

A:. Office worker?

Q: Yes.

A: Yes.

Q: How many office workers that you pay a salary?

A: I think it is seven.

Q: Seven?

A: Yes, that is right.

The cross examination began with Solicitor Thetford asking King questions. It will be observed that he made frequent reference to the Minutes that I had taken on December 5 and December 8, as he questioned King. Below are some questions asked by Thetford and answers given by King.

Q: This bus boycott or bus protest, whatever you choose to call it, was call for the 5th of December through a series of little pamphlets—you are familiar with what I am talking about?

A: Yes, I am familiar.

Q: Is it true they appeared on the streets a day or two before the protest meeting concerning alleged grievances?

A: I really couldn't say. I don't know if the pamphlets were put out for more than one day. I just don't recall what the pamphlets said concerning the time.

Q: Those pamphlets were pretty well distributed over Montgomery?

A: Yes.

Q: Starting about Thursday or Friday before the 5th of December; is that true?

A: That is true, yes.

Q: I believe you and a group of other men met on Monday afternoon?

A: That is right.

Q: How many of you were there? If you like to, we have the Minutes of the meeting here for the purpose of refreshing your recollection. This is just a photostatic copy of them.

A: All of these persons were present. (indicating)

Q: Did you personally know all of them?

A: Oh, yes, sir.

Q: Refreshing your recollection, how many of them?

A: According to the Minutes, eighteen.

Q: After refreshing your recollection would you say there were substantially that number?

A: That is right. ...

Q: At that time you formed the Montgomery Improvement Association?

A: Yes, we did.

Q: You elected your officers?

A: Yes.

Q" Elected an Executive Committee too, I believe? Refreshing your recollection, "Moved and second that the sixteen person here"—the Minutes up here show eighteen present—"And a suggestion that nine names be brought in making twenty-five which constitutes the Executive Committee." Do you remember the Executive Committee of twenty-five with nine others to be named?

A: Yes, that is right. I remember that.

Q: Was it agreed at that time to set up the transportation and finance committee, names to be supplied later?

A: I don't know.

Q: Refresh your recollection with this. I don't know exactly what it means myself. On page 3 of these Minutes it simply shows transportation committee and finance. Can you explain what that means?

A: I don't know, and that really isn't clear enough for me to make any statement concerning it. I really don't remember about these committees.

Q: Let me ask you this. Did you have anything to do with what I will refer to as the first boycott, the boycott called for December 5th?

A: No. Do you mean if I had anything to do with calling it?

Q: That is right.

A: No, I didn't.

Q: Do you know who did?

A: No I don't. It was a spontaneous beginning, one of those

things which just had been smoldering.

Q: Do you know who printed those pamphlets?

A: No, I don't. ...

Q: I note in your Minutes of that first meeting "It was recommended that resolutions would be drawn up," and a Resolutions Committee was appointed?

A: Yes.

Q: You were on that committee, I take it?

A: I don't believe I worked on the Resolutions Committee. That committee was appointed.

Q: Your Minutes show "The president, Rev. M. L. King, Attorney Gray and Attorney Langford are on the committee." Is that true? They are your Minutes, aren't they?

Q: Who drew up that Resolution?

A: This committee, this Resolutions Committee.

Q: Who was on the Resolution Committee at the time?

A: I don't remember.

Q: When was the Resolution drawn up?

A: Sometime during the meeting at the Holt Street Baptist Church.

Q: You are telling the Court that the Resolution wasn't drawn up at the afternoon meeting, but it was drawn up that night; is that what you are telling us?

A: That is right.

Q: And it was also agreed at the afternoon meeting that the protest would be continued; is that correct?

A: I don't know.

Q: Let me read it to refresh your recollection, or you can read it.

A: Well, that is true according to the Minutes, according to the Minutes here. I don't remember the discussion at this point.

Q: You are familiar with the Resolution I take it?

A: Well, I have seen it.

Q: You have seen it?

A: Yes, I have.

Q: You stated you have never asked anybody not to ride the buses. Let me read you what the Resolution says. It says: "That the citizens of Montgomery are requesting that every citizen in Montgomery, regardless of race, color or creed, to refrain from riding buses owned and operated in the City of Montgomery by the Montgomery City Lines, Incorporated until some arrangement has been worked out between said citizens and the Montgomery City Lines, Incorporated." You say this was made up on that night. That is what the Resolution says.

A: I didn't read the Resolution.

Q: You heard the Resolution read?

A: This was done by the committee. Oh, yes.

Q: You were there?

A: Oh, yes, sir.

Q: Who read the Resolution?

A: My best recollection, Rev. Abernathy read the Resolution.

Q: Rev. Abernathy?

A: Yes sir. ...

Q: In other words, what the Montgomery Improvement Association did, as I understand it, is to back an existing one-day boycott and by this the protest, or whatever you want to call it, has extended over a period of several months and it is still in existence; is that substantially true?

A: Yes and no. The last part is true, it is still in existence. Now, as to the first part I would say the Montgomery Improvement Association came into being in an attempt to improve the general status of the city plus the—

Q: That is not in response to my question at all.

A: I was fixing to give the other part of it.

Q: That wasn't responsive to my question.

THE COURT: ASK IT AGAIN.

BY THE SOLICITOR:

Q: I ask you this: I said the Montgomery Improvement Association, as I understand it, backed an existing one-day boycott and has through its transportation committee and others urged people not to ride the buses, and that situation is still existing today?

A: No. I wouldn't say so.

Q: Isn't that the way it came about?

A: No. ...

Q: How many white members have you at this time in the Montgomery Improvement Association, to your knowledge?

A: I really don't know. We don't keep records of those by race.

I couldn't say how many white members we have.

Q: How many do you think that are members of the Montgomery Improvement Association that are white?

A: Well, I don't know. I know Rev. Graetz is a member, and we probably have some others. I know we have some others.

Q: Who are they?

A: I don't recall at this point. ...

Q: Coming back to the Minutes of your first meeting, "It was passed that the recommendations from the committee be given to the citizens at the night meeting." That is right, isn't it?

A: That is right. ...

Q: As a matter of fact, you remember being at this organizational meeting on the afternoon of the 5th?

A: Yes, sir.

Q: Did you draw up this agenda for the meeting that night on the afternoon of December 5th?

A: I don't remember for sure when that was drawn up.

Q: Look at this right here and you read that. (indicating)

A: I imagine so, that it was drawn up there.

Q: Were you at a meeting of the Montgomery Improvement Association December the 8th, 1955?

A: I don't remember. What was the nature of the meeting?

Q: I am referring to the Minutes of the meeting and it says the contact committee of the Montgomery Improvement Association.

A: The contact Committee.

Q: The contact Committee.

A: I don't see anything about a contact committee. I don't know about it.

Q: I am reading from your Minutes.

LAWYER SHORES: We object to that from whose minutes?

SOLICITOR: They are the Montgomery Improvement Association Minutes that are in evidence.

THE WITNESS: I didn't write these.

THE SOLICITOR: Take a look at your Minutes and see what they say.

LAWYER BILLINGSLEY: You are using "your" and "we" sometimes. "Your." You are using your organization.

THE SOLICITOR: I take it is his organization.

BY THE SOLICITOR:

Q: Look at it and see what it relates to and give an answer to my question.

A: I am not familiar with that name. I guess that is the name the secretary used. However, that committee was appointed by the Executive Board.

Q: By the Executive Board?

A: Yes, sir.

Q: That is the Executive Board of the Montgomery improvement Association?

A: That is right.

Q: That is the committee that met with Mr. Thrasher, Rev. Hughes, the bus officials and the City Commission?

A: That is right.

Q: On December 8th?

A: Yes, I think that is the date. ...

Q: You say that the contact committee, of which you were a member, was appointed by the Executive Committee?

A: That is right. ...

Q: How much money have you in your bank account over in Atlanta now?

A: I really don't know.

LAWYER SHORES: We object to the wording of the question "In your bank account."

THE COURT: He has already said he don't know.

BY THE SOLICITOR:

Q: Let me change that. You have a bank account in the name of the Montgomery Improvement Association in the Citizens Trust in Atlanta?

A: That is right, we do.

Q: Now, I believe that $5,000 was deposited in that bank in Atlanta, the same $5,000 you drew out of the Alabama National Bank?

A: That is right. ...

Q: On February 21st do you know what the amount was you had put into bank?

LAWYER SHORES: We object to that. It has nothing to do with this case.

THE COURT: Overrule your objection. The reason I am going to let it in, this is money spent by the Montgomery Improvement Association and collected for the purpose of helping out with the so-called boycott. For that reason I will let it in.

LAWYER SHORES: The amount wouldn't make any difference.

THE COURT: Show how much they collected at that time. He said voluntary contributions were given for the purpose of aiding the boycott.

LAWYER SHORES: We concede money was collected and put in the bank.

THE SOLICITOR: We would like to know the amount.

LAWYER SHORES: This is fishing.

THE COURT: Overrule your objection.

LAWYER SHORES: We take an exception.

(Exception noted for the defendant.)

BY THE SOLICITOR:

Q: Do you know?

A: No, I don't know.

Q: I believe that you have stated that the Montgomery Improvement Association is being run on a budget of about $3,000 a week?

A: Well, approximately that.

Q: The Montgomery Improvement Association is spending approximately $400 a day? I wouldn't say exactly, but it might be in that area.

Q: And whatever is being spent by the Montgomery Improvement Association, so far as you know, is being spent for the continuance of the protest or boycott?

A: Well, I don't know exactly what you mean by the continuance of it. When you say continuance, I don't exactly know. (King's testimony concludes).*

*TD. Transcript, "State of Alabama v. M. L. King, Jr., No. 7399" (Court of Appeals of Alabama, 1956), 482-507: Copy in AAGR-A-Ar: SG 8423.

On Thursday afternoon, March 22, Judge Carter brought the four-day trial to a close, announcing the verdict; guilty as charged. King was fined $500 plus court costs or serve a year at hard labor. King's attorneys announced they would appeal, and King was freed on a $1,000 bond. Newspapers recorded the exact moment, 4:39 p.m., when King emerged from the courthouse to tell a cheering crowd that the bus protest would continue. King declared that "This conviction and all the convictions they can heap on me will not diminish my determination one iota. He also said, "We will continue to protest in the same spirit of nonviolence and passive resistance, using the weapon of love." Judge Carter orders a continuance in the other cases until final appeals are completed in King's case. The following day King's attorneys began the formal appeals process.

On that Thursday night at the mass meeting held at the Holt Street Baptist Church, King announced that the boycott would continue. He urged the people to keep up their spirits despite his conviction. Realizing that there were people in that audience who had all but lost faith in the American system of justice he said, "Let us not lose faith in democracy. For with all of its weaknesses, there is a ground and a basis of hope in our democratic creed." We all left that meeting inspired by King's hopeful message and more determined to continue the protest than ever.

We had experienced an outpouring of support from people across the nation. One example of this would be seen in the ten thousand people who came to the Gardner C. Taylor's Concord Baptist Church in New York on that Friday night, March 25, when King traveled to New York for the first northern speaking engagement since he became a front-page figure. At that rally, sponsored by the Brooklyn Chapter of the National Association of Business and Professional Women's Clubs, when the collection plates were passed the people contributed $4,000 for the support of the Montgomery Bus Boycott. Additionally, pledges of financial contributions were made.

Ten years after the King trial in Montgomery where I was a star witness for the State of Alabama, I was on trial in California, charged with having violated sections 3383 and 3381 of the Sierra Madre City Code as a result of my having performed a religious ministry in that city where the attitudes of whites were similar to those of whites in Montgomery. What I had learned in Montgomery during the King trial, not the least being to stand up and fight for justice, emboldened me for my trial in California.

In my trial, Judge John Henry W. Shatford handed down a 20-page decision on January 20, 1966, following the effective defense by my lawyer, Attorney George Baltaxe, that exonerated me from all charges Sierra Madre had registered against me and three of my fellow-missionaries who were members of the American Missionary Society, an auxiliary of the American Christian Freedom Society, an organization that I had helped to found a year after I left Montgomery and moved to California and was its president. This is a brief on the trial:

In the Municipal Court of the Pasadena Judicial District County of Los Angeles, State of California
The People of the State of California (Plaintiff)
vs.
Uriah J. Fields, Suniez Leveain Todd No. M 74254 and 74252
Nathaniel Ball and Johnnie F. Cameron No. M 74253 and 74255
(Defendants)
CONCLUSION:
"Sections 3383 and 3381 of the Sierra Madre City Code, as construed and applied to the defendants are unconstitutional, being in contravention of the Fourteenth Amendment, which Amendment embraces the liberties guaranteed by the First Amendment. The shotgun attempt to cover total divergent matters by the draftsmanship of the City of Sierra Madre Code Sections hereinabove set forth create a vehicle for monstrous abuse of the constitutional liberties which cannot be tolerated.
The defendants are ordered discharged.
Dated: January 20, 1966
Judge Henry W. Shatford.

Determined to convict me and my colleagues, the City of Sierra Madre appealed the Judge's decision. This was the result:

In the District Court of Appeal of the State of California
Second Appellate District—Division One:
The People of the State of California
Plaintiff and Appellant,
v.

Uriah J. Fields, et al CR A 6799 MO 74254 CR A 6931 MO 74252 Defendants and CR A 6932 MO 74253 CR A 6933 MO 74255 Respondents

"The record on transfer in the above entitled cause having been filed in the Court on September 2, 1966 pursuant to certification made by the Appellate department of the Superior Court of Los Angeles County, and this Court having considered the matter of whether such cause should be transferred to this Court for hearing and decision, now, therefore, it is hereby ordered that such transfer be and it hereby is denied."

Filed September 12, 1966
J. T. Alley, Deputy Clerk

King, the MIA leader, had been tried and found guilty of leading an illegal bus boycott in Montgomery. To repeat, he had been ordered to pay a $500 fine, plus $500 court cost or spend 386 days in jail. His lawyers had announced that they would appeal his conviction and he was free on $1,000 bond. The charges against eighty-nine other MIA leaders who had been arrested on the same charges as King were still in the court's charge. The black community, and black leaders in particular, found some consolation in the fact that a considerable number of people, black and white, across America were now, since the trial, financially supporting the boycott. The MIA leaders were especially gratified and encouraged by the generous financial support people were giving to the MIA. Nevertheless, there was a sense of pessimism that loomed heavily over black people in Montgomery. We realized that the white establishment would not cease their efforts to crush the boycott, humiliate the boycotters and destroy boycott leaders. We anticipated the unleashing of some other wrathful act upon us at anytime, but we did not know what form it would take. At this stage of the boycott, the white people of Montgomery were more desperate than ever before. They feared that the federal court might favor blacks in bus desegregation just as they had done in the case of Autherine Lucy when the court ruled that she must be admitted to the University of Alabama. From the beginning of the boycott we had seldom known what to expect. We had frequently been unpleasantly surprised by something horrible such as bombings, shootings, the new Ku Klux

Klan march in the black community, city officials announcing their membership in the White Citizens Council and threats from city officials aimed at coercing black people into ending the boycott without any change being made to improve the condition of black bus riders. Time and time again we had also been surprised by joy. Sometimes that joy resulted from the aforementioned evil acts. Our adversaries had meant it for evil, but it produced good like King's trial, that caused people who did not live in Montgomery to become a part of black Montgomerians' struggle for justice. But we did not know what the future would bring. We only had the hope that we shared with each other, particularly during mass meetings and in sharing rides.

On March 27, Alabama Attorney General John Patterson filed a motion urging dismissal of the "Browder v. Gayle" federal suit against Montgomery and Alabama transportation segregation laws on the grounds that the case should be held in a state court first. Two days later and just one week after the trial, the MIA held a mass meeting at the Hutchinson Street Baptist Church. King presided over the meeting. After greeting the people, he introduced me to sing a song that I had composed. He told the people that I had shared this song with him and that he felt they should also hear it. He added, "It certainly expresses my feeling and commitment to this bus protest." I told the audience that the title of my song is, "No Turning Back." Then I proceeded to sing it. About time I started singing the second stanza it seemed that everyone in the audience was singing it with me. These are the words to this song:

We are boycotting Montgomery buses,
We are boycotting Montgomery buses,
We are boycotting Montgomery buses,
No turning back, no turning back.

We are determined to keep on walking,
We are determined to keep on walking,
We are determined to keep on walking,
No turning back, no turning back.

Not 'til we get a bus ride to justice,
Not 'til we get a bus ride to justice,
Not 'til we get a bus ride to justice,
No turning back, no turning back.

On April 2, the Montgomery City Commissioners denied the MIA's request for permission to establish and operate a black-operated bus company. That night at a mass meeting held at the Beulah Baptist Church, King presented the MIA's voter registration plan that would be used in the soon-to-be-launched voter registration campaign. This was the first time voter registration had been on the MIA agenda. And I had not heard a black leader publicly discuss voter registration in the context of developing and executing a plan that would be put into effect to register blacks to vote since Nixon ran for commissioner prior to the boycott. At the time it was very difficult for a black person in Montgomery to register to vote even when he attempted to do so.

The good news in early April was that money, and lots of it, was being sent to the MIA. King, Abernathy and Nixon were all engaged in fund-raising. I did some, but being in Graduate School I had a limited amount of time to devote to fund-raising. Nearly all of my fund raising was done locally. In general, black people were waiting for something to happen that would cause them to return to riding the buses and hoping for a breakthrough. On April 23, the news came that in "Flemming v. South Carolina Electric and Gas Company," the Supreme Court affirmed a federal appellate court ruling striking down segregated seating on buses in Columbia, South Carolina, and making segregation on any public transportation illegal. Upon receipt of the news, Montgomery City Lines announced that its drivers would no longer enforce segregation, effective immediately. The black folk in Montgomery were about to announce that the bus boycott had ended when Mayor Gayle angrily announced that the city would continue to enforce segregation on the city buses. C. C. Owen, president of the Alabama Public Service Commission, stated that the court's ruling was for South Carolina and did not apply to Alabama. The National City Lines' legal vice-president, B. W. Franklin, stated that the company would stand behind any driver whom the city tried to prosecute. That evening we held a mass meeting at Dexter Avenue Baptist Church. The small auditorium was able to accommodate only about one-third of those who attended the meeting. King stated that we did not know what to make of the Supreme Court ruling in the South Carolina case as far as what effect if would have on us returning to the buses in Montgomery. He suggested that we wait for additional information on this matter. The next day bus lines in thirteen southern cities, including Dallas and Richmond, discontinued segregation on their buses. On the same day, we held an executive board meeting that focused on the Supreme Court ruling in the South Carolina case and what should be our response to it. Some board members felt that we should return to the buses on a desegregated basis, despite the mayor's reaction to the decision. Again, the majority of the board members felt that we should wait at least another week before returning to the buses. On Thursday, April 26, the mass meeting was held at the Day Street Baptist Church where a vote was taken favoring us continuing the boycott. Most of the 3,000 people attending that meeting asked black leaders to urge the city to withdraw its threat to arrest drivers and prosecute passengers who violated Montgomery's bus segregation laws.

At the last MIA mass meeting for the month of April that was held at the Holt Street Baptist Church, King acknowledged that there had been no new development regarding city officials' reactions to blacks riding the buses on a desegregated basis. He spent much of his time seeking to boost the morale of boycotters that had noticeably plummeted since the South Carolina decision. The leaders of the protest were acutely aware that their people were asking of them something more than just encouragement to continue the boycott. On the first day of May, Montgomery City officials filed suit in Montgomery Circuit Court asking for a temporary injunction to restrain the bus company from implementing its announced desegregation policy. In response to the demurrer filed the next day by Montgomery City Lines, a day later Judge Walter B. Jones ruled that Montgomery and Alabama segregation laws were constitutional and ordered Montgomery City Lines to abandon its new policy of not enforcing segregation. A spokesman for the bus company announced that they will comply with the order. On May 11, a three-judge U. S. District Court panel heard the "Browder v. Gayle" case. Judge

Richard Rives, Seybourn Lynne, and Frank M. Johnson, Jr. heard testimony by city and state officials, employees of the bus company and the four black women plaintiffs. The panel of Judges reserved their decision. The black folk in Montgomery did not know whether or not they would rule in their favor or how long it would take for them to rule.

Some boycott leaders were greatly concerned about the inadequacy of the car pool. People were complaining more than before about not being picked up at the scheduled times and the cost of operating the car pool had skyrocketed in the last two months even though a fleet of twelve 1956 station wagons had been added to the transportation system. These station wagons, partly donated by automobile companies, were assigned to churches. Printed on each side of each station wagon was the names of the church and pastor of the church that a particular station wagon had been assigned. One of these station wagons was assigned to the Bell Street Baptist Church where I was the pastor. My church was also a pick-up and dispatch station. In an attempt to limit the abuse of over-charges made by some drivers and some leaders of the car pool who found this to be an easy way to siphon off funds from the car pool operation for their own personal benefit, the executive board chose Benjamin Simms to be supervisor of the transportation system. This did not solve the problem because the same leaders, Lewis, Glasco and Seay were calling the shots just as they had done before. Moreover, Simms was ill-prepared to serve in that position. Soon Simms was accused of gouging and misplacing car pool funds. In the face of being terminated, he resigned. Some people, including those named above, benefitted financially from their involvement as operators of the car pool. One month the cost of operating the car pool exceeded $7,000, up from its usual $5,000, even though the quality of the service rendered had deteriorated.

During the early weeks of the boycott the weekly expenses of the MIA was $2,500. Beginning in late January the cost had increased to $3,000 just before King's trial in mid-March. With more money coming into the treasury after the trial the MIA car pool expenses increased substantially. By late March the cost of operating the car pool was $5,000 a week. In addition, another $1,300 was spent to operate the office and pay employees. At the peak of the protest, around mid-May, the MIA spent $8,500 a week to operate the car pool and for administration. Not included in this amount was the money that speakers usually received to pay for their transportation. Additionally, there were the honorariums speakers received. And some equipment and furniture paid for by the MIA ended up in places other than the MIA's office.

The Franklyn W. Taylor, Jr. "MIA Audit Report, 1 March to 31 May, 1956," hastily issued on June 25, 1956, two weeks after I publicly accused some MIA officials with having misappropriated funds, stated that the MIA received $220,848.87 by May 31 and had expenses of $104,312.41 during that period. The report also stated that the MIA had a balance on March 1 of $6,444.07. In his book, "Parting the Waters" (p.188), Taylor Branch stated that "at the time of the court victory, MIA had stowed away deposits totaling more than $120,000 in banks from New York to Oklahoma—outside of Alabama and therefore safe from legal raids by Attorney General Patterson." In the booklet "Dr. E. D. Nixon, father of the Civil rights Movement: A Forgotten Hero" ((p.6), Nixon), treasurer of the MIA, stated that he raised more than $100,000, begged five cars and two vans and had $60,000 dropped into his door's mail slot." I stated in my book, *The Montgomery Story: The Unhappy Effects of the Montgomery Bus Boycott* (p. 36), "According to the most reliable sources, approximately $100.00 cannot be accounted for, while nearly another $100,000 is at present presumably deposited in banks in several states."

Obviously, Franklyn W. Taylor did not have sufficient data in 1956 to do an accurate "crash-calculation" audit for the MIA. A more accurate figure as to the total sum of money the MIA had received by May 31, the day I expressed to the executive board members for the last time my dissatisfaction with the way MIA funds were being handled would be $403,245.87 rather than $220,848.87. At that time Nixon was not able to make an acceptable or accurate treasurer's report because he did not have the information such as receipts and expenditures, needed in order to make such report. The MIA's financial controllers wanted Nixon to be a fund-raiser and check-signer, nothing more. He was temporarily appeased or, at least there was an attempt made to appease him, by the board's decision to pay his travel expenses and reimburse him for the money he spent in raising funds. Nixon made it known that he felt that some of the funds that some speakers kept as honorariums should have been turned over to the MIA.

Nixon, the treasurer and I, the secretary, were not given certain financial information. The justification for withholding it from us was that this refusal to provide us with this information would enable MIA to keep it out of the hands of the white establishment who otherwise would get our records just as they had done for the trial. I often felt that King wanted, in some way, to hold me responsible for him being found guilty at the trial because the court had used my secretarial records in that trial. I do recall that subsequently when the government investigated his payment of income taxes, that he publicly stated that I had been responsible for the actions taken by these tax investigators. I do not feel that there was one shred of evidence to support his claim. There was never a time when I wanted white people to have access to the MIA's financial records. Because I plan to say more about the finances of the MIA in the next section when I discuss, "Why I Resigned as Secretary of the Montgomery Improvement Association," suffice that I say nothing more about the funds collected and spent by the MIA in this section.

During the May 31 executive board meeting, King asked that funds be allocated for a voters registration project that would be directed by Lewis, who I feel benefitted financially more than any other person from the MIA. However, there were others who also benefitted financially from the MIA. In support of his recommendation for funding the project King said: "The key to the whole solution of the South's problems is the ballot. Until the colored man comes to this point he will have a struggle. When he gets the ballot, he can wield political power and come into his own. ...The chief weapon in our fight for civil rights is the vote."

We all agreed with King as to the importance of the vote. I realized how difficult it had been for me to become a registered voter the first year I was in Montgomery and I recalled then as I had done on previous occasions the effort I had personally put forth after I became a registered voter in assisting students at Alabama State College in their preparation to register to vote. I had mentioned these things to my fellow-executive board members more than a few times. However, I vigorously opposed appropriating money to that project under Lewis' charge. However, over my objection the executive board accepted King's recommendation and authorized him to use such funds as he determined necessary to get the voters registration project started. He was asked to report back to the board in a month on the status of the project. At the time that report was due, I would no longer be a member of the MIA's executive board.

On June 1, Attorney General Patterson, drawing strength from a Louisiana Judge's orders of the prior April 24 that ordered a permanent halt to all NAACP activities in that state, obtained a court order banning most NAACP activities in Alabama. The injunction, issued by Judge Jones of Montgomery Circuit Court, forbade the Alabama NAACP from engaging in fund-raising, collecting dues, and recruiting new members. The NAACP denied Patterson's charges that it organized the Montgomery bus boycott or employed Autherine Lucy to integrate the University of Alabama but said it would abide by the injunction. When the NAACP rejected a corollary order to surrender its membership and contribution lists to Patterson, the judge imposed a $100,000 contempt fine as well. Despite the NAACP's legal expertise, including having Thurgood Marshall, who later would become a U. S. Supreme Court justice, as head of its legal team, it took that organization eight years, more than one-seventh of the length of time it took that organization and other parties with similar interests to successfully argue the "separate but equal" doctrine before the Supreme Court that was ruled to be unconstitutional. Moreover, neither Patterson nor the State of Alabama had to pay the NAACP one penny for their criminal conduct that deprived NAACP members of their First Amendment rights to be represented by people and organizations of their choice.

On June 5, blacks in Birmingham reacted to the banning of the NAACP by organizing, under the leadership of the Rev. Fred Shuttleworth, the Alabama Christian Movement for Human Rights. Shuttleworth, pastor of Birmingham's Bethel Baptist Church and the most courageous black leader in Birmingham would demonstrate time and time again during the next decade that he had no fear of that City's white racists, chief among them being Police Commissioner Eugene "Bull" Connor who gained notoriety for having turned fire-hoses and dogs on black marchers that included women and children. That same day the good news came that the three-judge panel ruled two-to-one in the case of "Browder v. Gayle" that segregation on Alabama's intrastate buses was unconstitutional and gave lawyers for each side two weeks to submit written suggestions on how the formal anti-segregation order should be entered. President Owen of the Alabama Public Service Commission announced that the state would appeal the decision all the way to the Supreme Court. The boycott continued.

Just as the first six months of the boycott was about to end with segregation on buses continuing to be the practice in Montgomery, the U. S. States Court of Appeals had declared that segregation on buses in Montgomery was unconstitutional, thus making it the first time in history of the State of Alabama that such had been done by a court. The Kings and the Abernathys having received this good news and with the MIA being financially secure, they left Montgomery by automobile for a vacation in California where they first stopped in Los Angeles. I had just finished the third quarter in graduate school at Alabama State College and was hard at work writing my master's thesis in the hope that I would receive my master's degree in education in mid-August.

Little did black Montgomerians realize in early June 1956 that we had traveled only one-half the distance of the boycott journey that would lead us to a "bus ride to justice" in Montgomery. For me, in a certain way, it would be the end of my boycott journey, but not the end of my leadership in Montgomery and my fight to secure justice and integration. I would keep on singing "No Turning Back," but not as a member or officer of the MIA. I was convinced that, at this point, the best way that I could contribute to the bus boycott was to simply not do or say anything for it or against it. I would continue to live in Montgomery until the boycott ended, and blacks returned to riding city buses, integrated buses, and several years after King and Abernathy permanently moved to Atlanta.

PART THREE

The Last Half of the Montgomery Bus Boycott

Midway through the three hundred and eighty-two day long Montgomery Bus Boycott, on June 11, 1956, during a mass meeting at the Beulah Baptist Church, I charged some boycott leaders with malfeasance and announced that I was resigning, effective immediately, as the secretary of the Montgomery Improvement Association, an organization that I, Martin Luther King, Jr., E.D. Nixon, Ralph David Abernathy and fourteen other persons had formed six months earlier, on the first day of the bus boycott, to serve as the vehicle that would be used to direct and manage the bus boycott.

King, Abernathy and their wives, Coretta and Juanita, respectively, had left Montgomery by automobile the next day after receiving the good news on June 5th that a panel of three federal judges had ruled in a two-to-one decision in the suit that had been filed by Attorneys Fred Gray and Charles Langford back in February asking the court to rule that the Montgomery bus segregation ordinances were unconstitutional. Attorneys for the city and Alabama immediately appealed that decision to the U. S. Supreme Court and the boycott continued. Like other black people in Montgomery King and Abernathy were gratified by the decision and it seemed to them that there had not been a better time since the boycott began to take a short vacation. It was also a time when there was more money in the MIA treasury than ever before. The court decision was an indication that the slowly grinding mill of litigation in the courts did sometimes produce justice for black people. All the previous decisions the courts had ruled on pertaining to the bus boycott had favored the white segregationists, not black justice-seeking people. Even this decision that declared bus segregation to be unconstitutional in Alabama was an attempt to undue a wrong and infamous decision that had been made by the U. S. Supreme Court in the "Plessy v. Ferguson" case in 1896, some sixty years earlier, which held that "separate but equal," hence segregation and jimcroism, were constitutional. Despite unjust rulings made by the courts, black people never ceased to look forward, not backward, and with hope that they would receive more justice in the courts which they themselves were for the most part excluded from other than as being subjects, oftentimes victims, for the courts to try, convict and sentence.

As King, Abernathy and their wives journeyed to California where they anticipated spending two weeks vacationing, things were somewhat calm in Montgomery with black people awaiting the next happenstance. Based on their experience, since the boycott began, that would occur any day, very soon. Shortly after King and his companions arrived in Los Angeles they received word from the MIA office in Montgomery and later from the news media that I had publicly charged some MIA leaders with misusing MIA funds and resigned as the secretary of the Montgomery Improvement Association. In his crafty-couched and fury-spiced statement to the news media, King denied that MIA funds had been misused and said that I had been terminated as the secretary of the MIA. Of course, he did not speak the truth on either account. Back in Montgomery, Lewis and Seay, both members of the MIA executive board, also denied that MIA funds had been misused, and another board member Rev. A. W. Wilson said that he was not aware that any funds had been misused and emphasized that he had not personally handled MIA funds.

Some people expressed the belief that I had waited until King and Abernathy left Montgomery to bring my charges so that I could increase my chance of staging a leadership coup. Taylor Branch writes in *Parting the Waters*, (p. 189): "By timing his gambit to coincide with the absence of King and Abernathy, Fields hoped other disgruntled leaders would rally to demand a restructuring of the executive board." The fact is, before I learned that King and Abernathy were leaving the city and going on their vacations, about a week before they left, I had concluded in my own mind that in early June I would go public with my allegations about the misuse of

MIA funds and resign as the secretary of the organization. Nearly two months before making these charges, I had told members of the executive board that I did not approve of the way MIA funds were being used and that the withholding information on the finances from the secretary and treasurer was unacceptable. I had made it clear that I felt that the treasurer, Nixon, not the financial secretary Erna Dungee, should give the financial report to the executive board. Nixon had said more than a few times that he did not have sufficient information on the finances, especially as to how they were being dispensed, to make the treasurers report. I had also questioned the appropriateness of some allocations of funds that were made in the interest of certain individuals, not in the interest of the operation of the boycott. Moreover, before King and Abernathy left on their vacation, I had been divinely directed by Him, who never ceases to be my Light and Salvation, to make the charges I made and to resign as the secretary of the MIA.

Admittedly, I had underestimated the degree of loyalty black people had for King. But after I made my charges and resigned as the secretary, I soon learned that they had much more respect for King than they had for me, notwithstanding the fact that I came to Montgomery nearly two years before he did and had been a pastor of the Bell Street Baptist Church in the city a year before he became pastor of the Dexter Avenue Baptist Church. And, I had also worked with Nixon, Jo Ann Robinson and other black leaders with the objective of advancing the black agenda in Montgomery before he came to the city.

At that June 11 mass meeting, I also stated that "Some MIA leaders had become too egotistical and interested in perpetuating themselves," and that "I can no longer identify myself with a movement in which many are exploited by the few." It was my experience with the MIA that had led me to say what I said at that mass meeting. I had observed selfishness that manifested itself in the way some leaders were selected or permitted to fill speaking engagements. Some leaders, other than King, would speak only in large cities where they would be likely to receive bigger honorariums than would in towns and rural areas. The endeavor of some members of the executive board to correct this practice did not succeed, mainly because some of the most influential leaders continued to choose the places they would speak and disallow others from speaking to those audiences. As I stated earlier I did very little speaking outside of Alabama because I did not want to take time away from my graduate studies.

To deal with this problem, the executive board appointed Rev. H. H. Johnson as chairman of the five-member Speakers Bureau, but when he was unable to make decisions without interference from some of the leaders who continued to select the places they would speak, he resigned from the Bureau which he said was nothing more than a sham. Abernathy demanded that he, like King, be permitted to select the places where he would speak. This did not go over well with the members of the Speakers Bureau. Some leaders felt that Nixon should not be permitted to speak before large gatherings because he used bad grammar. Instead, it was felt that he should talk to individuals and leaders of corporations where he was effective in raising funds. I opposed any attempt to exclude Nixon from speaking in the larger public arenas.

Some leaders were class-conscious with a strong need to be popular. This desire to be popular caused certain leaders to misbehave in an attempt to draw attention unto themselves. I know of instances when some leaders used MIA funds to purchase advertising so they could get their names and pictures published in the newspaper. Doing a mass meeting, one MIA leader who had been designated to be the main speaker, upon not seeing a reporter present just minutes prior to the hour he was to speak, called the Fire Department, not because there was a fire, but to draw attention to himself. He succeeded, when firemen came but found no fire. The next day it was noted in the newspaper that this leader had urged the people to remain calm while firemen checked the church but found no fire. It is unbelievable as to what some people will do to draw attention to themselves. I would sometimes criticize some leaders for their narcissistic behavior. Fanfare and sensationalism embraced by some of these leaders accounted for increased hardships that resulted in some people experiencing increased pain and making a volatile situation more volatile.

The lack of MIA leaders to take measures to prevent the Communists from infiltrating the protest movement was another reason why I decided to resign as secretary of the organization. I received only minuscule support from leaders in my endeavor to keep the Communists out of the Montgomery movement. Only Rev. A. W. Wilson agreed with me that the Communists posed a threat to the protest and that we should take measures to keep them out of it. Nixon was of the opinion that "we should accept help from anybody who wanted to help us." I could understand these leaders' lenient disposition toward the Communists, but I felt strongly that one of the MIA's priorities should be establishing a defense against Communist infiltration into the Montgomery movement so as not to jeopardize the effectiveness of the leaders. Although I heard King say more than once, "We are using Christian principles that are opposed to Karl Marx's damaging revolution method," and, on one occasion, "One of the things that we have insisted on throughout the protest is that we steer clear of any Communistic infiltration," he did not demonstrate to me that he was seriously concerned about wanting to keep the Communists out of the Montgomery movement. Even as I urged the leaders to work to keep the Communists out of the protest, I recognized that keeping them out would not be easy. The U. S. Government was aware that keeping the Communists out of the Government could be difficult. The Government, empowering Senator Joseph McCarthy by making him chairman of the House on Un-American Activities and financing its operation, was a failed attempt by the Government to deal effectively with Communism in the United States. That attempt was obviously destructive, not so much to the Communists, but to a large number of Americans, especially for those whose lives and careers were ruined as a result of being defamed by that Committee. I felt that keeping Communists out of the Montgomery movement was something that black leaders needed to do in order to remain viable. There were also some other black leaders outside of Montgomery who were concerned about MIA leaders keeping free of the Communists.

On March 5, about two weeks following the indictment of King and nearly eighty-nine other boycott leaders in Montgomery, Leonard G. Carr, treasurer of the National Baptist Convention, informed King that he was turning over $151 to the Baptist Ministers Conference of Philadelphia and that it would be forwarded to the MIA. He went on to give King this advice, "...whenever you are invited to speak for civic movements, be sure that they are not on the subversive list." Continuing he said, "It was called to my attention that the Rev. Ralph D. Abernathy is to speak for the Civil Rights Congress in these parts. If I recall correctly, they have been placed on the subversive list." In 1953, the Civil Rights Congress was the first of twelve organizations to be cited as Communist fronts by Attorney-General Herbert Brownell. The subversive Activities Control Board ordered the CRC in December 1955, the month the boycott began, to register with the Attorney-General and submit to that agency information about their membership, finances, and its primary activities. I recall that I had to fight hard and long to force King to return a contribution to a Communist organization. I did convince him not to deposit the check in the bank, but he refused to return it to the donor until another organization that had pledged to give a sizeable donation to the MIA, upon my urging, informed King that it would not donate unless the contribution made by the Communists was returned. Faced with that reality, King returned the contribution to the Communist organization. I could understand King and some other MIA leaders, including Nixon, being willing to take financial help from the Communists, especially in light of the fact that the Ku Klux Klan and White Citizens Council, greater enemies to black people than the Communists, financed those who opposed the boycott, but I did not want King to suffer the same fate that Paul Robeson had experienced after he was charged with being a Communist or a Communist sympathizer by the House on Un-American Activities. President Truman ordered his passport lifted. King permitted a friend of Rustin's and a longtime official of the American Jewish Committee, a man who had heavily financed the Communist Party during the height of the Joseph McCarthy era, to become involved in the Montgomery movement. He told executive board members that "Comrade STP" had to be all right because he was highly respected in Jewish circles. In my retort, I reminded King and others present of what had happened to Jewish Julius and Ethel Rosenberg who had been convicted and executed in Sing Sing after being charged with giving atomic secrets to the Soviet Union. Single-handedly I succeeded in ejecting this Communist out of the Montgomery protest movement. However, it was becoming increasingly clear to me that I would not be able to single-handedly keep the Communists out of the Montgomery movement.

But the main reason that I resigned as secretary of the MIA was because of the misuse of MIA funds by some MIA leaders. As I stated earlier, according to the "MIA Audit Report," that was issued on June 25, just two weeks after I charged some MIA leaders with misusing funds and resigned as the secretary of the Association, the MIA had raised, as of May 31, 1956, a total of $220.848.87 and spent $104,312.41. The report also stated that the MIA had a balance on March 1 of $6,444.07. According to this report at the end of May, there was a balance of $116,536.46. Based on my secretarial records $30,000.00 was unaccounted for and there were doubts in the minds of some leaders, other than myself, as to whether or not the amount of money that had been reported to be in banks at the time was, in fact, in banks. The MIA secretary had been denied some information on bank transactions on the pretext that withholding such information from him would make it difficult for the courts to access the MIA's financial records and, more importantly, to freeze or confiscate funds held by the organization. I agreed that there was the probability that the courts might freeze or even take MIA assets and approved of the MIA board authorizing one of its executive board members to deposit MIA funds in an out-of-state bank in his name so that the MIA would have financial resources to operate, should the white establishment freeze or take funds the MIA had in banks. However, I did not feel that any of these concerns justified the withholding of information about MIA finances from the secretary and, in some instances, the treasurer. Members of the executive board also agreed that all cash money received should be held and not deposited in the bank so that it would be readily available for emergency purposes, especially in case the court froze the MIA bank accounts.

Later, when I was no longer secretary of the MIA, at a court trial held about a month before the boycott ended, Judge Carter of the Montgomery Circuit Court declared that he was considering issuing an injunction to halt the car-pool and impose a $15,000 fine on the MIA to compensate the City of Montgomery for lost of tax revenue that resulted from the Montgomery Bus Boycott following a surprise witness's testimony which revealed that the MIA had on deposit $189,000 in his Montgomery bank. This information was supposed to have been private, but black people had few rights that white people respected. This was reminiscence of the famous Dred Scott decision of 1857 in which the United States Supreme Court affirmed in that decision that Negroes had no rights that white people were legally bound to respect. Time and time again, the private affairs of black people were put on public display in Montgomery.

From my collaboration with Nixon and two other boycott leaders, I feel safe in saying that $150.000 was unaccounted for and a significant percentage of the money spent for the operation of the car pool went into the pockets of people who were neither drivers or owners of cars that were used to transport those boycotting buses. Rip-off money were received by some people who paid the drivers, gasoline service station owners, and those who repaired vehicles used in the boycott. The owner of one garage where MIA vehicles were repaired told me that he gave kick-back money to the person who paid him for his service and added, "I don't mind doing that because he pays me well." I contended that this money would have been better used had it been used to help needy people who were hurting because of the boycott.

I was not opposed to compensating some MIA workers for their service. As a matter of fact, I proposed that King be paid a monthly stipend. Most board members opposed doing that and King did not go along with the idea. It was agreed upon that King be allowed to keep honorariums that were given to him for speaking. I had a problem with that even though the majority of the board members approved of that procedure. Nixon wanted to know where did honorariums end and funds for the MIA begin? That question was never answered to the satisfaction of Nixon or myself. The answer given was, in paraphrase, "We can trust King to do what is right." Maybe, in that regard, King would do what was right, but when such was expected of some other leaders there could be a problem. I most definitely could not agree with using that method to compensate some of those who would be entitled to receive financial compensation from the MIA. To me that was not a proper way to compensate MIA leaders. I knew that some MIA leaders could not be trusted to keep their hands out of the cookie jar, so to speak, even when being watched by a non-collaborating party. Neither did my effort succeed to persuade MIA leaders to establish a benevolence fund to help people who were enduring hardship as a result of the bus boycott. Nixon and I did succeed in getting a commitment from the executive board to financially assist Rosa Parks when she fell on hard times after losing her job and, besides, she was married to a mostly underemployed and sometimes unemployed husband who drank too much, to put it mildly.

A member of the Bell Street Baptist Church where I was the pastor, a widow and mother of three children, ages 13, 11 and 8, came to my church office one day in distress. She had been fired the day before from her job by the family she had worked for as a maid for twelve years. Tearfully she said, "They fired me because I wouldn't ride the bus to work." She had been fired from her job just three days after Mayor Gayle went on television and criticized white women for being chauffeurs for their Negro maids. This mother of three, and the sole bread-winner in her home said to me that day, "I don't know how I am going to pay for my rent that is due next week or buy groceries, but I am not going to ride the bus until we get what we want." She was committed to the struggle and there were many others like her who suffered because they chose to not ride the buses. Hundreds were fired and some were given traffic tickets and harassed by policemen unjustly. Typically, a policemen would order a driver to push down on his brakes, open the trunk of his car, turn on his lights and verbally assault him in an attempt to make him angry and spur him to become defiant or violent. Yet many dedicated people, in the same spirit possessed by this widow, chose to not ride the bus until some measure of justice would be granted to bus riders. The MIA should have been there to assist those who experienced financial difficulty in meeting their basic needs. It is true that there were some instances when the MIA helped needy people to buy food and pay rent. And, sometimes the MIA referred needy persons to a particular church or pastor who helped them, but the organization could have done much more in this regard had this concern been considered one of its priorities.

It was on the last day in May during an executive board meeting when I decided that I was going to let the public know about the misuse of MIA funds and resign as secretary of the organization. That very night an angel appeared unto me and instructed me to speak the truth that I know about the misuse of MIA funds and resign as secretary.

It was on June 11 that I publicly stated at a regular weekly mass meeting, held at the Hutchinson Street Baptist Church, my knowledge of and disapproval of the manner in which MIA funds were being misused and resigned as the secretary of the MIA. Immediately after taking this action, I became to black people the Benedict Arnold of the Montgomery Bus Boycott movement. Some white people were delighted that I had exposed some black leaders as undesirable representatives of black people and resigned as the MIA secretary. Other white people, convinced that I was an integration leader, were not eager to embrace or applaud me for having made charges against some MIA leaders and resigned as the secretary of that organization. They did not feel that I would cease fighting for integration. Some of them were aware of the fact that when King had been calling for what NAACP director Roy Wilkins called "polite segregation," meaning that black and white people would remain segregated on buses but blacks would receive courteous treatment from bus drivers, I was calling for integration and that I was a registered voter. The latter being something that only a few of Montgomery black leaders had accomplished. Mississippi white supremacist J. K. Vardman spoke for most white people in Montgomery when he said earlier in that century: "I am just opposed to Booker T. Washington (and they would say Uriah J. Fields) as a voter, with all the Anglo-Saxon re-enforcements, as I am to the coconut-headed, chocolate-colored, typical little coon, Andy Dotson, who blacks my shoes every morning."

Despite all these things, my most direct adversaries or enemies were black people. To repeat, I had underestimated black people's loyalty to and admiration for King. Ever since I arrived in Montgomery, nearly two years before King came to the city, I had been on the firing line, insofar as taking a stand for black liberation was concerned. That included my fight to become a registered voter and my joining with Nixon in the pursuit of justice for black people. At this mid-point junction of the boycott, and nobody at the time knew that was the case, not anything that I had done mattered with the vast majority of black Montgomerians. They were suddenly oblivious of any positive thing that I had done since I came to Montgomery.

On June 14, the news spread like wild fire that I had been shot by members of my own race. Close to midnight the sounds of screaming sirens could be heard and two fire trucks, an ambulance and three police cars came to my home. It had been reported that the ex-secretary of the MIA and an alleged traitor of black folk had been killed and his house fire-bombed. Of course, I had not been shot nor had my house been set afire, but without question there were people who wanted me dead. Now, some blacks whom I had taken to be my friends had forsaken me. I could not walk down the streets without having people say, "There goes that traitor!" Or "What is the Mayor paying you?" Or "You better leave town before sundown!" I requested police protection, but I never received it. I learned how to literally sleep with one eye open and one eye closed. I kept my pistol and shotgun within arm's reach when I was home. I had not taken the vow to be nonviolent as had some black leaders and I was not about to change my view with regards to defending myself. It was out of my experience at that time that I wrote this poem, "In Defense of Myself":

> The Greek Oracle Socrates said
> "Know yourself."
> Kierkegaard said, "Choose yourself."
> Surely, we have all heard,
> "Self-preservation is the first
> law of nature."
> I have but one life and it is precious
> unprecedented and never to be
> repeated.
> It is all that I have.
> Conscious of the enemies of my life
> I stand ready at any moment
> to act "in defense of myself."
> I will not surrender my life to any
> scavenger or murderer without
> a fight to the finish.
> And, I will employ any weapon that
> will help me to remain alive.

I must reiterate that I had not anticipated black people becoming as hostile toward me as they did. Yes, it was King, not I, who they confided in and trusted to provide them with Moses-style salvation and lead them to the Promised Land. I questioned the unwisdom of my actions and wished, even as I realized the futility of such wish, that I could turn the clock back prior to June 11, but I knew that could not be done. So, I pondered as to what I could do, but no answer came, at least no answer indicating anything that would help me to be restored back to the family-like relationship I had with black Montgomerians prior to this incident. I felt alone, forsaken, somewhat like an abandoned child and, even worse, my life literally hung in the balances.

On Monday, June 18, I met with King shortly after he, having cut short his vacation in California, returned to Montgomery upon hearing the news that had spread from coast to coast about the charges that I had made about leaders misappropriating MIA funds and my resigning as the secretary of the MIA. I came to his parsonage, located at 309 South Jackson Street, that morning after having talked with him on the telephone about a hour and a half earlier. During our telephone conversation I told him that I would like to come and talk with him in person. He seemed pleased from the tone of his voice and ready to have me talk with him. Later, when he opened the door to let me enter his home, the expression on his face revealed a pleasant countenance; however, I would soon learn that he was furious about the statement I had released to the press, and he told me so, in no uncertain terms. No sooner than he closed the door he said, "God damn you! Why in the hell did you put our business in the streets?" he shouted. He expressed his concern that white people would use what I had said to defeat the bus protest and that we would lose everything that we had worked, fought and suffered for over these past six months. Then I told him remorsefully that I had no intention of hurting the Montgomery Bus Boycott and attempted to convince him that I did not feel that he had personally misused any MIA funds. I added that I felt some other leaders had misused MIA funds. He responded, "You are probably right." And said, "You dealt with this matter in the wrong way. This was an in-house matter that should have never been told to anyone other than members of the executive board." Then I told King that I wanted to come to the mass meeting tonight and let the people know that the press had misunderstood what I had said. King wanted to know if I would retract what I had said and offer an apology to MIA leaders and to the people boycotting the buses. I explained to him that I would deny everything that the press had claimed I had said about the misappropriation of funds. Then I told him that I want to offer my resignation as the secretary of the MIA. To my latter statement, he responded, "Are you sure that you don't want to remain secretary of the MIA?" He added,"I think that if you continue to serve as the secretary it will help the public to feel that we are a united people." Convinced that I was determined to resign as the secretary of the MIA, he did not press the matter any further. Then with a sorrowful countenance I said, "I will see you at the mass meeting," and left his home with ambivalent feelings.

The June 18 mass meeting was held at the Beulah Baptist Church. When I arrived at the church that evening it was over-filled with hundreds of people outside who could not get inside the church. When King and I entered the sanctuary, everything was quiet...quieter than I could ever remember things being at the beginning of a mass meeting. There were angry looks on the faces of a lot of people in the audience. King and I took our seats on the rostrum. Rev. W. F. Alford, pastor of this church, in a subdued tone of voice, said, "You are now in the hands of the president." For a moment after King came to the lectern, there was continued silence both by him and the people in the audience for about a minute. Then King greeted the people. His mood was somber, and somewhat grave. Before he could say anything more someone in the audience asked, "What is that traitor doing sitting up there with you Rev. King?" That was followed by mumbling and grumbling from quite a few people. Dr. King disregarded the question and the mumbling and grumbling and said, "We have a serious problem. You all know that Rev. Fields made some accusations to the press a week ago charging some MIA leaders with having misappropriated MIA funds. Now, I don't know anything about the misuse of any MIA funds. I have talked with Rev. Fields earlier today and he is here to make a statement concerning this matter. Someone in the audience retorted: "He said it! I heard him say it!" Rev. King rose and said, "Rev. Fields is here and we would like to hear from him. Let us listen to what he has to say." As I approached the lectern I was greeted with boos from quite a few people. Rev. King stood again and said, "Let us hear him. Let him speak." I began by reciting a poem that I no longer can remember except I know that it contains these words:

Others Lord,
Yes, others.
Let me live for
Others Lord.

Continuing, I said, "Yes, a week ago I said that some MIA funds had been misused by some MIA leaders. Tonight I want to say that what I said was not true...it was not true. It was out of personal hurt, disagreement between myself and some MIA leaders that led me to charge some MIA leaders with having misused funds. I never said that Dr. King misused MIA funds. I want to say as I speak to you remorsefully and with a hurting heart that I do not have any evidence that MIA leaders have misused MIA funds. I retract everything that was reported in the press about the misuse of MIA funds. As you know, I have supported the bus boycott from day one, and even before the boycott began, I worked along with Nixon, Jo Ann Robinson, my pastor, Rev. Johnson and others in trying to make life better for us in Montgomery. I would not knowingly do anything to interfere with the successful outcome of the bus boycott. I offer my apology to Rev. King, the leaders of the boycott and to each one of you for having made untrue statements about the way funds have been misused. That was not the truth. I ask for your forgiveness." At that point I was overcome with deep emotions as tears literally rolled down my checks and I took my seat.

King said, "Rev. Fields has shown courage and expressed remorse for what he said about the misappropriation of MIA funds. We don't have to always be right; but we do have to get right, or at least we should. Rev. Fields has made a real effort here to get right. Before coming to this meeting he contacted me in person and said that he wanted to come to this meeting and make a statement to correct what he had said. He did this freely, without myself or any other person, as far as I know, having asked him to do so. Now, he has retracted what he said about the misuse of funds by MIA leaders. I think, in the spirit of the Christ who we call Lord, that we should forgive Rev. Fields. I want to see a show of hands of those who are willing to forgive Rev. Fields." About two-thirds of those present raised their hands. It was apparent that the remainder of those present were not willing to forgive me, if indeed all those who had raised their hands truly forgave me. I continued to see anger in the faces of a lot of people in that audience. Nevertheless, I was glad that I had been granted the opportunity to speak at that mass meeting and got a somewhat favorable response.

King and I had made this joint appearance and I had retracted what I had said to the press about the misuse of funds by some MIA leaders and King had publicly forgiven me and asked others to do likewise. Both King and I had done a "public thing," the expedient thing to do, for the good of the bus protest and probably for the good of each other. In a certain way, we had both won. But I had the feeling immediately after that mass meeting that King had voted with that third of the audience who did not raise their hands when he asked the people to vote to forgive me. I believe that time has proved that my feeling was correct. However, on the night of that mass meeting we both had much at stake. My life was at stake and the effectiveness of King's leadership was at stake. The charges that I had made against MIA leaders could have subjected the MIA to scrutiny by the courts had I maintained that the statement I made to the press was true. King and I left that meeting without expressing any comrade-like or brotherly interest in each other. We both had received from each other what we wanted, at the time, maybe, what we needed from each other. Never again would I meet face-to-face with King even though we both remained as pastors in Montgomery; he until January 30, 1960 and I until July 7, 1962.

The day following that mass meeting the news media reported that I had retracted my statement about the misuse of MIA funds by MIA leaders. That news release did not send out the shock waves as had my original statement charging MIA leaders with having misused MIA funds. News about human shortcomings and misdoings, even when they are untrue, gets more attention by news reporters and readers than good news. Oftentimes good news is no news. Some reporters expressed the opinion that I had been coerced into retracting my original charges against some MIA leaders, but they offered no evidence to validate their claim. They admitted that no MIA leader had stepped forward to collaborate their assumption.

I retracted my statement primarily because I did not want to do anything that would interfere with the continuation of the bus boycott, even though I knew that I would no longer actively participate in the bus boycott. I had resigned as the secretary of the MIA and severed my relationship with King and most other MIA leaders. I say "most," because I never ceased to have a cordial relationship with some MIA leaders, including Nixon. Privately some MIA leaders said to me, "Fields, we know you told the truth when you said that MIA funds had been misused by some MIA leaders." But I knew that I was finished with that issue even though it was clear to me that that issue had not finished with me. I decided that henceforth I would not express a view either for or against the boycott. However, I did continue to speak out for justice and the advancement of black people. About a year after I left the Montgomery Improvement Association, I founded the Montgomery Restoration and Amelioration Association through which I worked to address non-boycott issues blacks faced in Montgomery. A few of the achievements of MRAA were: influencing the City to put side walks on Oak Street that were used by a large number of students who attended Carver High School, prompting the employment of the first black cashier in a medium-size supermarket in the city, and persuading a downtown general department store to employ the first black person to be employed as an assisting manager in the city.

My troubles stemming from my breaking away from the Montgomery Bus Boycott did not end with me making a retraction statement. Many blacks, perhaps most, continued to hold ill-will against me. Not least among them were some preachers who did everything in their power to encourage members of the Bell Street Baptist Church to oust me as their pastor. Several of those ministers had a portion of my church membership to hold an unauthorized business meeting for the purpose of voting me out as their pastor. Following the meeting, some of these disgruntled members changed the locks on the doors of the church to make sure that I could not enter, they thought. But it didn't work. While I was preaching one Sunday, I noticed that an unusual fear was upon the congregation, but I did not know what the uneasiness was all about. Members were disturbed because they had been informed that a county sheriff and a deputy were outside of the church waiting to arrest me and take me to jail. A wicked member of my congregation, George Durden, had been influenced by outsiders to swear out a warrant for my arrest. That he did. On that Sunday, when I had finished preaching, as soon as I walked outside of the church I was arrested on a disorderly conduct charge and taken to jail. Once at jail I was booked, fingerprinted and released on a bond posted by one of my members, Mrs. Carrie B. Cooper, who operated a private school. I had ordained Durden to be a deacon in Bell Street Baptist Church a year earlier. It reminded me of Jesus who had chosen Judas to be a disciple. This was a humiliating experience for me. Never before had I been in a jail except to visit or minister to others in prison, with one exception; while serving in the Army, I spent a brief time in the stockade when military policemen discovered that I did not have my furlough papers with me. I was not absent without leave as they insisted on believing. I had left my orders at my mother's home. Loyal Members of the Bell Street Baptist Church flocked to the jail following my arrest and some of them remained there until I was released from jail. Their concern about my welfare gave me the encouragement I needed to face the challenges that were just ahead and beyond.

Coupled with my arrest was an attempt by certain ministers in the city and some members of the Bell Street Baptist Church to oust me as pastor of Bell Street Baptist Church by any means necessary, including litigation. Rev. H. H. Hubbard, pastor of the Bethel Baptist Church, encouraged my members to take me to court and promised them that he would pay the court cost. Some uncooperative members spurred into action with outside of the membership support, filed an injunction aimed at forcing me out as pastor of Bell Street Baptist Church with the claim that I had been voted out by the membership and was no longer their pastor. I was summoned to appear in Montgomery's Circuit Court, but my accusers were disappointed when Judge Walter B. Jones refused to issue an injunction. Instead, he ordered that a vote of the membership be taken, under the supervision of a master approved by his Court and accepted by members who were for me remaining their pastor and those who were opposed to me being the pastor of Bell Street Baptist Church. Subsequently, members loyal to me gave me a majority vote. After that about a fifth of the members left Bell Street Baptist Church and joined other churches in the city, including Hubbard's Bethel Baptist

Church. This would by no means be the end of my ministry at the Bell Street Baptist Church or my leadership in Montgomery. I would continue to be a factor to be reckoned with in Montgomery. My presence remained strong. However, I decided to devote my time and energy to being a pastor, including rebuilding the church's membership, and to my studies. At the time, I was beginning the last quarter in fulfillment of the requirement for my master's degree in education. Some of the teachers at Alabama State College who had previously greeted me with smiles and offered me words of encouragement were now shunning me. Some of them would look in another direction when passing me. One of my graduate school professors, L. D. Reddick, whose full name is Lawrence Dunbar Reddick, a person who I, then secretary of the MIA, had provided information on the inside workings of the MIA when he was writing his book, "Crusader Without Violence: A Biography of Martin Luther King, Jr.," sought to persuade me to quit school and leave Montgomery. He had suggested this, I believe, in good faith and well-meaning. He told me that my burden was too heavy to bear and expressed the opinion that it may be possible for me, the person he referred to in his book as a "rising shining star," to shine in some other place away from Montgomery. I told him that I would think about what he had suggested. When I talked with him after class three days later I again expressed to him my thanks for his concern about my welfare and informed him that I plan to remain in college and in Montgomery. He said, "Fields, I know that you are a fighter and you will do what you feel is best." I had the clear feeling or, maybe it was a thought, that some of my teachers might choose to give me bad or even failing grades, despite the fact that I had made excellent grades previously. But to their credit and scholarship integrity and in recognition of my scholarly performance they gave me the grades that I deserved, all A's except for one B, similar grades to those I had received in the preceding quarter.

As I reflect on that moment in my personal history when I was just beyond my mid-twenties, I have no regrets for the way I lived my life. I do not feel that I could have lived it differently. There has never been a time, except for brief moments, when I was not convinced that a Power far greater than myself was in control of myself, directing my behavior, and I have had the distinct feeling that my good was never overlooked by Him who created everything good. Sometimes I have said I came here for such a time as this so that I could do what I am doing. I remain aware now as I did during the Montgomery Bus Boycott that I had then and have now a message to deliver that is mine alone to deliver and that nobody else, be he ever so great, can deliver the message I have been sent to deliver. And until then, until time for me will be no more, I will keep on delivering my message.

Following my break with the bus protest movement, financial contributions to the MIA dropped considerably, according to MIA treasurer, Nixon. More than a few people outside of Montgomery, including some who derided me publicly were, nevertheless, convinced that the charges I had made against some MIA leaders' misuse of funds were true. In a letter to Bayard Rustin, dated September 20, a little more than three months after my break with the Montgomery movement, King writes:

> At present our finances are holding up fairly well, however, in the last two or three months our out-of-town contributions have dropped down tremendously.

However, funds that had been raised before I resigned from the MIA, along with other contributions in smaller amounts than had been received during the first six months of the bus boycott from out-of-state and those made by people in Montgomery, were sufficient to cover expenses for the remainder of the bus boycott with some money to spare. It just may be that one of the good things that resulted from my calling attention to the spending practices of the MIA was that the leaders began to assume more fiscal responsibility that resulted in the MIA, just one month before the bus boycott ended, having $189,000 in a Montgomery bank and an undisclosed amount in at least two out-of-state banks.

The saddest thing for me about this whole dramatic episode or debacle is that after the night when I attended a mass meeting and retracted my statement about the misappropriation of funds by some MIA leaders and King asked the people present at that mass meeting, the last one that I would attend, to forgive me, is that he and I never reached out to each other, not so much as to meet face-to-face again. Before his death twelve years after this event we never forgave each other. Maybe, just maybe, King did forgive me, but if he did, I never had any way of knowing that because he never put forth the effort to contact me and let me know. I suppose he could say I forgave him on the night he made his retraction statement. I do know that when I attended his funeral in Atlanta in April of 1968 I had not forgiven him. But like many thousands who had gathered to mourn his death I, too, was sad and in great pain. But two years after his death I forgave King, and when I did, a heavy weight was lifted from my soul. I cannot say with any certainty, I can only hope that King forgave me. I realized much too late, to be sure, that forgiveness is more important for the forgiver than it is for the forgiven. I now confess that I waited much too long to forgive King. For that I have paid a price. "Thank God Almighty, I am free at last."

Some days before the Civil War, Theodore Parker, an abolitionist preacher, said to people who were no less impatient than the people of Montgomery, "The arc of the moral universe is long, but it bends toward justice." "Toward justice." That was the direction in which time was moving for bus boycotters in defiance of segregation laws and with a resolve to suffer and persevere to help bend the arc of the moral universe "toward justice."

In July and August there was a quietness in Montgomery unlike what had been since the boycott began. The car pool, consisting of twenty-four church station wagons and one hundred cars in full-time service and a greater number of people using their cars voluntarily, part-time or anytime to help others in need of rides, continued to transport 20,000 people daily. The people's resolve to not ride the buses remained in tact and they kept faith and hoped that justice would come to the buses in Montgomery. However, when that would happen no one could predict.

On August 10, I received a Master's of Education degree from Alabama State College. For me this was a significant achievement. I had become the first member of my family to receive a Master's degree, not withstanding the fact that four of my sisters were teachers. During my time in graduate school, especially the last one-and-a-half quarters, I was under tremendous pressure. It was a kind of pressure that I had never experienced before, not even when I was in the military. I felt that I was hated by many people close to me. Despite that, I had devoted myself to study and was able to finish near the top of my class. Equally as important, I had been emboldened by my achievements and I sensed that I possessed an invincibleness that is best expressed in these words from a song that says, "Ain't no power on earth can keep me down."

On August 25, several sticks of dynamite exploded, damaging the home of Rev. Robert Graetz, the white pastor of a nearly all black congregation. Returning home that day he discovered that not only had his home been bombed, but his records and correspondence had been confiscated by police as part of the bombing investigation. While he was being interrogated by detectives his two-year old son shouted, "Go away, you bad policemen!" Papa Gaetz later confessed that a surge of pride came over him on hearing those words from his pugnacious son. Some white people in Montgomery never ceased to believe that Graetz was the brain and chief strategist behind, even if not before, the bus boycott because in their minds they could not accept the fact that black people could, as one white person told one of my church members, "outfox white people."

Two weeks later, September 8, several insurance companies succumbed to the pressure from the White Citizens Council and announced the cancellation of policies covering seventeen of the twenty-four station wagons used by the MIA car pool. That meant that these vehicles could not be used in the car pool until they could be insured. Other insurance companies also refused to provide coverage for these vehicles. It would be two months, one week and five days, November 20, before, with the assistance of an Atlanta insurance company, the MIA received a Lloyd's of London Policy, retroactive to September 18, that insured each of these vehicles in the amount of $11,000. During that period when these vehicles were not insured, people continued to ride in other vehicles that were in the car pool and in "share-a-ride" vehicles provided by volunteers who wanted to assist boycotters needing rides. But more people had to walk to reach their destinations than at any other time during the boycott.

Still craving for knowledge and feeling the need to spend time away from Montgomery even while remaining in Montgomery, the second week in September I enrolled at the Gammon Theological Seminary in Atlanta. (The year I graduated the Gammon Theological Seminary, I joined with several other seminaries to form a federation that constituted the newly established Interdenominational Theological Center). Gammon Theological Seminary awarded me a three-year scholarship. One of the things that made continuing my education at Gammon Theological Seminary even more attractive was that I could leave Montgomery on Monday and return on Friday. The seminary had a challenging curriculum and scholarly teachers. During my three years at the seminary I was privileged to take two courses, one on leadership, under the tutorship of the seminary's president, Dr. Harry V. Richardson, a course that greatly impacted me, probably more than any other course that I can ever remember taking. I got off to a good start during my first semester at the seminary, excelled in my studies and graduated "cum laude," third in my class. What I learned in seminary about theology and philosophy has meant more to me than words can convey, even when I attempt to use philosophical and theological terminology to declare my intentionality.

In late October the news came that a car pool injunction was imminent. On November 1, in response to the possibility of a court injunction against the MIA car pool, boycott leaders submitted a petition in the U. S. District Court for an injunction and restraining order to prevent the city commissioners' effort to seek an injunction against their car pool. Later that night, Montgomery city officials, as expected, delivered a petition that asked Judge Eugene W. Carter of the Montgomery Circuit Court, for an injunction to halt the MIA car pool. The next day, also as expected, Judge Carter scheduled a hearing for November 13. In the meantime, Judge Frank M. Johnson of the federal district court denied the motion by MIA representatives for an emergency restraining order to prevent Montgomery city officials from interfering with the operation of the MIA car pool and set a hearing for November 14, one day after Judge Carter would hold a hearing on the city commissioners request.

On Thursday, November 13, Judge Carter listened to city lawyers urge him to ban the MIA car pool. They also asked that he impose a $15,000 fine on the MIA to compensate the city for loss of tax revenue. Judge Carter granted an injunction halting the MIA car pool. The following day Judge Johnson refused to interfere with the enforcement of the state injunction halting the car pool operation. At this point the troublesome waters were continuing at high tide, almost overpowering, but not quite. The road ahead for bus boycotters looked bleak, indeed. But black people of Montgomery had learned from mistreatment and some painful experiences that "when the waters are troubled, that is a good time for a miracle to happen." Would a miracle happen at that particular juncture when most of the station wagons used in the car pool had been grounded and there were more tired feet than at any other period during the boycott? Only time would tell and it seemed as if time was running out for the bus boycotters. But a miracle had already happened that the bus boycotters didn't know about.

As destiny would have it, the same day Judge Carter granted the City of Montgomery a temporary injunction banning the car pool, a miracle happened. The U. S. Supreme Court affirmed the lower court opinion in "Browder v. Gayle" that declared Montgomery and Alabama segregation laws unconstitutional. The Supreme Court had announced that decision a few hours before Judge Carter issued his injunction, but King, like others in that courtroom, did not know about the Supreme Court's decision until late morning during court recess when an Associated Press reporter, Rex Thomas, came to the front of the courtroom and handed him a note that contained a bulletin he had torn off the AP ticker that read, "Dateline Washington. The United States Supreme Court today affirmed a decision of a special three-judge panel in declaring Alabama's state and local laws requiring segregation on buses unconstitutional." The Supreme Court had acted without listening to any argument: it simply said, "the motion to affirm is granted and the Judgment is affirmed."

I had just finished my last class for the day in New Testament Studies at the Gammon Theological Seminary when a classmate, William C. Dobbins, also a pastor of a Methodist Church in Montgomery, told me that he had just heard that the Supreme Court had ruled that bus segregation in Montgomery was unconstitutional. A feeling came over me that I had not had since the day I had received my voter's registration certificate about a year after I took up residence in Montgomery; and then again, I recall that I had a similar feeling when I received the news on May 17, 1954, that the Supreme Court had ruled in the "Brown v. Board of Education of Topeka" that "separate but equal" in education was "inherently unequal" and that school segregation is unconstitutional. Although I had not encouraged black folk to boycott buses since I severed my relationship with the MIA and King, six months ago, I had strongly urged people prior to that to boycott the buses and I had never ceased hoping and praying that the boycott would succeed in the desegregation of buses in Montgomery. So with this Supreme Court decision, I joined in rejoicing with 50,000 other black Montgomerians and some white Montgomerians, although I would not venture to say how many white Montgomerians. And I expressed my gratitude to God for having directed the Supreme Court justices to make the decision that banned bus segregation in Montgomery. When I returned to Montgomery the next day from Atlanta, I found black people rejoicing. However, later that day, bus manager Bagley announced that segregation would be enforced until the May injunction the city had obtained against the bus company was dissolved. That evening, two simultaneous MIA mass meetings were held, one at the Hutchinson Street Baptist Church and the other one at the Holt Street Baptist Church. Three thousand attendees at these mass meetings voted unanimously to end the bus boycott when the court mandate arrived. On Thursday, MIA leaders asked NAACP lawyers to take steps to request that the Supreme Court speed up the delivery of its order to Montgomery, in light of the injunction the city had against the MIA car pool. On the following day, Friday, November 17, Thurgood Marshall and three other attorneys asked Supreme Court Justice Hugo L. Black to hasten delivery of the mandate implementing the Supreme Court's November 13 decision. On November 19, Justice Black refused to expedite the order.

With the car pool banned and the Supreme Court's decision having not been formally delivered to Montgomery, the black community was in a precarious condition. Black folk took even more to walking than in the past. MIA leader Rev. Hubbard declared, "the court has no injunction against feet." Some leaders decided that they would walk for about a month to show solidarity with those who did not have access to automobiles. Others used their cars even more than they had previously to transport their neighbors and friends, discovering that they had more neighbors and friends than they had realized. There were many tired feet. One only had to listen to the words and look into the eyes of protesters to be convinced that their souls were at peace. Their songs were melodies that sounded like joybells ringing, not muffled drums.

While awaiting the Supreme Court's final order, the MIA held a week-long "Institute on Nonviolence and Social Change" that had been scheduled for December 3-9. The opening message was delivered by King at the Holt Street Baptist Church. He spoke on the subject, "Facing the Challenge of the New Age." Many distinguished people from across America attended the institute. Among them were Mahalia Jackson, Lillian Smith and Dr. J. H. Jackson, president of the National Baptist Convention. Dr. Jackson delivered the closing address of the institute on December 9 at the First Baptist Church. Much of the focus of the week was on preparing black people to ride on integrated buses in Montgomery.

Alabama's final appeal is rejected by the Supreme Court on December 17. The actual mandate arrived at Judge Johnson's office on December 20. That same day the U. S. Marshals delivered writs of injunction to Montgomery City officials. Judge Jones dissolved his injunction against Montgomery bus integration and rebuked the Supreme Court. That night the MIA held two mass meetings, one at Holt Street Baptist Church and one at St. John AME Church. King reminded the people to follow the "Integrated Bus Suggestions" that had been distributed to all present. A day before the Supreme Court's order arrived in Montgomery, the MIA leaders prepared this statement that was titled, "Integrated Bus Suggestions:"

This is a historic week because segregation on buses has now been declared unconstitutional. Within a few days the Supreme Court Mandate will reach Montgomery and you will be re-boarding INTEGRATED buses. This places upon us all a tremendous responsibility of maintaining, in face of what could be some unpleasantness, a calm and loving dignity befitting good citizens and members of our Race. If there is violence in word or deed, it must not be our people who commit it.

For your help and convenience the following suggestions are made. Will you read, study and memorize them so that our nonviolent determination may not be endangered.

1. Not all white people are opposed to integrated buses.
Accept goodwill on the part of many.

2. The WHOLE bus is now for the use of ALL people.
Take a vacant seat.

3. Pray for guidance and commit yourself to COMPLETE
non-violence in word and action as you enter the bus.

4. Demonstrate the calm dignity of our Montgomery
people in your actions.

5. In all things observe ordinary rules of courtesy and good
behavior.

6. Remember that this is not a victory for Negroes alone, but for
all Montgomery and the South. Do not boast! Do not brag!

7. Be quiet but friendly; proud, but not arrogant; joyous but not
boisterous.

8. Be loving enough to absorb evil and understanding enough to
turn an enemy into a friend.

NOW FOR SOME SPECIFIC SUGGESTIONS:

1. The bus driver is in charge of the bus and has been instructed
to obey the law. Assume that he will cooperate in helping you occupy
any vacant seat.

2. Do not deliberately sit by a white person, unless there is no
other seat.

3. In sitting down by a person, white or colored, say "May I" or
"Pardon me" as you sit. Ths is a common courtesy.

4. If cursed, do not curse back, but evidence love and good will
at all times.

5. In case of an incident, talk as little as possible, and always in
a quiet tone. Do not get up from your seat! Report all serious
incidents to the bus driver.

6. For the first few days try to get on the bus with a friend in
whose nonviolence you have confidence. You can uphold one another
by a glance or a prayer.

7. If another person is being molested, do not rise to go to his
defense, but pray for the oppressor and use moral and spiritual force
to carry on the struggle for justice.

8. According to your own ability and personality, do not be afraid
to experiment with new and creative techniques for achieving

reconciliation and social change.
   9. If you feel you cannot take it, walk for another week or two. We
have confidence in our people. GOD BLESS YOU ALL.
THE MONTGOMERY IMPROVEMENT ASSOCIATION
THE REV. M. L. KING, JR., PRESIDENT
THE REV. W. J. POWELL, SECRETARY

   That night, the night of the last Montgomery bus boycott mass meeting and on the eve of integrated bus riding in Montgomery, in Shakespearian fashion, black and some white Montgomerians exclaimed, "Tomorrow, and tomorrow, and tomorrow," and with the assurance of the Psalmist declared, "Weeping may tarry for the night, but joy comes with the morning." On tomorrow morning some black and white people will take their first integrated bus ride in Montgomery. They will take a "bus ride to justice" and claim the prize they walked for.

PART FOUR

Ride On! Ride On in Freedom

O Freedom, O Freedom, O Freedom over me!
Before I'll be a slave
I'll be buried in my grave,
And go home to my Lord
And be free.

"Ride On! Ride On in Freedom! A new day had dawned in Montgomery. After a 382-day long boycott of buses by black Montgomerians and a Supreme Court's decision that declared segregation on Montgomery buses unconstitutional, black people, joined by white people, would resume riding Montgomery buses.

At 5:45 a.m., on Friday, December 21, 1956, Rev. Ralph David Abernathy, E. D. Nixon, Rosa Parks, Inez J. Baskin, Attorney Fred Gray and Glenn E. Smiley gathered at the home of Rev. Martin Luther King, Jr., at 309 South Jackson Street in Montgomery. Seventeen minutes later, when the first bus of the day pulled up at a nearby intersection, Abernathy and Baskin took the first seats on the right of the bus and King and Smiley, a white man, who would be a party in the first integrated coupling to integrate the buses in Montgomery, took seats immediately behind Abernathy and Baskin. On the left side of the bus, behind the driver, other persons who boarded with King took their seats, beginning at the front of the bus. The bus driver greeted his passengers politely and said, "We are glad to have you ride on this bus." The photographers took pictures as the bus headed north on Jackson Street. At the next bus stop five more people, all were blacks, boarded the bus. They all took seats as near to the front of the bus as possible. Everyone on the bus was in good spirit but they showed no sign of celebrating. The driver went so far

157

as to make an unscheduled stop to pick-up Reverend Robert Graetz who greeted all aboard and said to Smiley, "You have already done it," inferring that Smiley had already integrated the bus by sitting beside King and, of course, parallel and to the right of some other black bus riders. Photographers on board took more pictures.

The following day I boarded a bus that traveled down Fairview, and for a while it passed through an all-white residential area. Three white people boarded the bus that had twelve black passengers who were seated in the front of the bus. Two of the three white persons took seats all the way back to the very last seats in the back of the bus and the other white passenger took a seat behind the blacks who were on the bus. After picking up eight other persons, the bus stopped downtown where Rosa Parks had boarded a bus 386 days earlier and was arrested about a hour later after she refused to obey the bus driver's order to give up her seat so that a white man could take it. I decided to leave the bus at that stop, even though I had planned to go to a store two blocks ahead. No sooner than I left the bus I heard people talking about a bus that had been fired upon that was traveling on the Cleveland Avenue route. That was the same route Parks had been traveling when she was arrested over a year ago. The good news was that no one had been hurt.

Early Sunday morning, on the next day, a shotgun blast was fired into King's home. The King family and his bodyguard were scared, but grateful that no one had been hurt. Violence in other parts of the city was also being reported. In response to an invitation that King had extended to him, Bayard Rustin arrived in Montgomery late Sunday morning. After taking a ride on an integrated bus, he visited King at his home and inspected the damage a shotgun blast fired into his home had done earlier that morning. He and King were happy to be together and even happier about integration on Montgomery buses being a reality. Rustin wanted King to know that despite the violence that had occurred the last few days, nonviolence would prevail. He emphasized that the important thing is that now integration on buses is the law. They discussed strategy for future progress in integration that would go beyond Montgomery.

Later that day Rev. M. L. King, Sr. arrived at his son's home. He had left Atlanta after he heard that his son's home had been fired upon. After greeting King and others present, he suggested, or, more correctly, commanded, that they join him in prayer. While he was praying a prayer that went on for a while, Rustin excused himself and went into another room. After praying, Daddy King, in a similar vain as his prayer, spoke of the need for prayer to assure God's favor and protection. King Jr. didn't seem to be impressed by what he had to say and they both began to be a bit confrontative in what they had to say to each other. After King, Jr. and Rustin talked again about strategy and what they felt would happen the next few days in Montgomery, Rustin departed from King's home.

Prior to delivering my sermon at the Bell Street Baptist Church that Sunday, I was told by one of my members that the Day Street route bus he had taken to church had been fired upon and all the passengers were ordered to leave the bus.

On Christmas Eve, a car pulled up to a Montgomery bus stop where a fifteen year-old girl was standing alone, and three white men jumped out of their car, flogged her, and quickly left the scene. The violence was not restricted to Montgomery. In Birmingham on Christmas Day the home of Reverend Fred Shuttleworth was bombed and almost totally demolished. Only a miracle prevented anyone from being badly hurt or killed, given the magnitude of the damage. But the next day Shuttleworth led three hundred of his followers into the white bus routes sections of Birmingham. Between Christmas Day and New Year's Day, snipers fired on several integrated buses in Montgomery. On the last day of the year, a volley of shots fired on an integrated bus hit a pregnant black woman, sending her to the hospital with bullet wounds in both legs and the right hand. City Commissioner, Parks, who at times extended a listening ear to black more than other commissioners, announced, to the dismay of black people, that the city would have to suspend bus service if the shootings continued. The question on the minds of Montgomerians was "What will happen from here?" The people I spoke to just prior to the New Year, including some white people, all agreed that bus integration had come to Montgomery to stay and, with few exceptions, they felt that both black and white people should accept bus integration and oppose violence.

During the first week of the New Year there were three incidents involving snipers firing on buses and one incident that involved a white man cursing and striking a black bus passenger. The black man did not respond violently. This would not be the end of segregationists' violent response to bus integration in Montgomery. Die-hard racists were determined to employ violence and prevent integration from continuing.

On Thursday morning, January 10 at 2:30 a.m., three weeks after buses were integrated, bombs exploded in six different locations in the black community of Montgomery that did considerable damage to four churches and two parsonages. The churches bombed were: Hutchinson Street Baptist Church, Reverend H. H. Johnson, pastor; First Baptist Church, Reverend Ralph David Abernathy, pastor; Mount Olive Baptist Church, Reverend E. D. Bell, pastor; and Bell Street Baptist Church, Reverend Uriah J. Fields, pastor. The parsonages bombed were those of Trinity Lutheran Church, Reverend Robert S, Graetz, pastor; and the First Baptist Church, Reverend Ralph David Abernathy, pastor. While all these churches and parsonages suffered significant damage, the Mount Olive Baptist Church and Bell Street Baptist Church sustained the greatest damage. As a matter of fact, Bell Street Baptist Church was the worst of the damaged churches. Regarding this point, Taylor Branch states in his book, *Parting the Waters*, (p. 200): "Bell Street Baptist Church suffered the most destruction on the night of the bombs." Except for Bell Street Baptist Church and Mt. Olive Baptist Church, the other churches and parsonages could be repaired. It was necessary to rebuild Bell Street Baptist Church, and Mt. Olive Baptist Church moved into other quarters.

I was in school at the Gammon Theological Seminary in Atlanta when a member of the Bell Street Baptist Church called and informed me early that morning that four churches and two parsonages, including the Bell Street Baptist Church, had been bombed in Montgomery. A fellow seminarian had just informed me minutes earlier that he had heard on the news that there had been bombings of several churches in Montgomery. About a hour later I left Atlanta and headed to Montgomery. When I arrived at the Bell Street Baptist Church around noon, a huge crowd had gathered at the site of the Bell Street Baptist Church, which was now literally in shambles. I was told by policemen at the scene that two bombs, not one, had been placed in the front and rear of the church building.

On Sunday, January 13, church members and others, including

sightseers and people who were just curious, gathered at the site of the church, now in ruins, for worship service. The worship service was held outside on the church property. The members of Bell Street Baptist Church and other concerned people at that service joined with me in pledging and committing ourselves to rebuild the edifice of the Bell Street Baptist Church. The National Baptist Convention, U.S.A., Inc., Rev. J. H. Jackson, President, and Rev. A. W. Wilson, representative for the interests of the aiding bombed churches to NBC, contributed $2,100 and the Reconstruction Committee for Bombed Churches, established by the Montgomery Improvement Association, contributed $6,000 to help rebuild the Bell Street Baptist Church. Despite the fact Bell Street Baptist Church suffered the most damage, First Baptist Church received forty percent and Mount Olive Baptist Church received thirty percent more funds from the Reconstruction Committee for Bombed Churches than the Bell Street Baptist Church. However, the members of the Bell Street Baptist Church were most appreciative to the National Baptist Convention, U.S.A., and the Reconstruction Committee for Bombed Churches for their financial assistance. The insurance carried by the Bell Street Baptist Church covered only the mortgage on the church. With these two contributions, a loan from a local bank and funds donated by members and friends, we were able to rebuild the edifice of Bell Street Baptist Church, although the church incurred a heavy indebtedness.

On Sunday, May 18, 1958, sixteen months after Bell Street Baptist Church was bombed, we had our entrance day, first service, in our new edifice. During the months following the bombing, until we rebuilt our edifice, the membership of Bell Street Baptist Church worshiped in the Trinity Lutheran Church school that was no longer being used by Trinity as a school. Carrie B. Cooper, a member of Bell Street Baptist Church, had rented the property and was using it for her own private school where she enrolled children in grades one through four. Indeed, this was a God-send for the members of Bell Street Baptist Church. Worshiping in this facility gave us the freedom we needed during this challenging period.

Five persons who confessed that they participated in bombing these churches and parsonages, including two of them who took the investigating detectives to the place where the unused dynamite had been disposed of, were found to be not guilty by a jury and acquitted by a judge, despite a preponderance of the evidence.

Two weeks after those bombings, just before dawn, on January 27, a bomb exploded on the corner street nearest to King's parsonage. A house and a black taxi stand were damaged. The taxi stand was fully demolished and windows were shattered in three taxis parked near the taxi stand, sending the driver to the hospital. Shortly afterward, twelve sticks of dynamite were found on the porch of King's parsonage. The policemen were able to remove these sticks of dynamite and defuse them before they exploded. A near riot erupted at the scene as blacks gathered at King's parsonage and expressed their dissatisfaction with the failure of policemen to act to prevent violence white people were inflicting upon black people. A few days later, seven young white men were arrested in connection with the series of bombings and other acts of violence.

The first month of bus integration in Montgomery had ended and most Montgomerians, black and whites, agreed that integration would continue and that all citizens and law enforcement people should do everything in their power to bring a cessation to the violence. With the passing of time, the violence did cease and bus integration became a part of the new integrated lifestyle in Montgomery.

As chief leader of the Montgomery Bus Boycott, King emerged as a national civil rights leader. Before he was assassinated in Memphis at the age of thirty-nine, he played a significant role in eliminating segregation, not only in the South, but throughout America. On the pages ahead we will discuss his legacy. Since the Montgomery Bus Boycott black people who no longer refer to themselves as Negroes, but as African Americans, or who I prefer calling Americans of African Descent, have achieved much and made great advancement since December 1, 1955, the day Rosa Parks refused to give her bus seat to a white man. The Black people in Montgomery responded by staging a bus boycott that continued for over a year and until the U. S. Supreme Court ruled that segregation on Montgomery buses was unconstitutional. On December 21, the boycott ended and blacks resumed riding the buses, this time integrated buses. What then can we say? "Ride On! Ride on in Freedom!"

Ride on! Ride on in freedom! Ride on until we,
the descendants of King and Queens but also
the descendants of slaves, develop to our fullest
potential and live life in freedom and with dignity.
Ride on! Ride on in freedom! Lift high freedom's light
and let it shine. Let it shine with a high beam
everywhere so that others may see it.
Ride on! Ride on in freedom! Extend compassion
and help those who are unfree to become free.
Ride on! Ride on in freedom! Proclaim that freedom
is not free, that freedom can be lost, and that the
price of freedom is eternal vigilance.
Ride on! Ride on in freedom! Sing a song of
freedom. And sing it like you never sung before.
Sing it over and over again. Sing it joyfully and
sing it with soul-power.
Ride on! Ride on in freedom!
Let freedom ring!
Let freedom ring!
Ride on! Ride on in freedom!
Ride on! Ride on in freedom!

EPILOGUE

In a Nutshell: The Legacy of Martin Luther King, Jr.

What did Martin Luther King, Jr. bequeath to humanity that continues, even into the third millennium, to cause people to revere him and embrace his legacy? This is the question that this writer, who considers himself to have been King's first civil rights secretary, proposes to answer in this "Epilogue." But before answering that question I want to present some relevant biographical data about King.

King was born on January 15, 1929 to Alberta Williams King and Martin Luther King, Sr., in the City of Atlanta, where he attended public school and earned his bachelor's degree at Morehouse College. He received a bachelor of divinity degree from Crozer Theological Seminary in Chester, Pennsylvania and a Ph.D. degree from Boston University. On September 5, 1954 he became the resident pastor of Dexter Avenue Baptist Church in Montgomery, Alabama.

On Monday, December 5, 1955, four days after the arrest of Rosa Parks on December 1, on charges that she had violated the segregation laws of Alabama by refusing to give up her bus seat to a white male bus passenger, King and seventeen other Montgomery leaders organized the Montgomery Improvement Association to be the organization that leaders would use to plan and conduct activities that would promote and manage the Montgomery bus boycott that had begun that very day, about eight hours earlier, before the MIA was formed. During the organizing meeting of the MIA, King was elected to be its president. As leader of that organization, he went on to provide leadership for the 382-day long successful bus boycott that ended after the U. S. Supreme Court ruled that Montgomery's and Alabama's bus segregation laws were unconstitutional.

Subsequently, King was the principal founder and president of the Southern Christian Leadership Conference. For more than a decade SCLC conducted sit-ins, freedom rides, voter registration campaigns, staged marches, including the August 1963 March on Washington. Nearly one-third of a million people gathered at the Lincoln Memorial to hear King deliver a speech that has become as endearing to many Americans as President Abraham Lincoln's "Gettysburg Address." At a later time, King protested America's involvement in the Vietnam War. He was jailed many times for having participated in civil-disobedience demonstrations. King was in Memphis participating in a Sanitation Workers' protest when he was assassinated on April 4, 1968, allegedly by James Earl Ray. Ray, who was given a life sentence for the crime, but until his death some twenty years later, never admitted that he killed King. There are many other people, including King's wife Coretta Scott King, who believe that Ray did not kill King, but that a conspiracy was responsible for his death. Some of those who believe that it was a conspiracy that killed King include Ray in the conspiracy, but others contend that he was not involved in King's assassination.

King was selected as *Time Magazine's* "Man of the Year" in 1956, awarded the 1964 Nobel Peace Prize and the United States Congress and the President approved the National Martin Luther King Jr. Holiday. Although King had many other achievements, it is now clear that he contributed magnanimously, noteworthily and praiseworthily to the advancement of African Americans and in making America a better place for all Americans. His fame has spread throughout the world.

What then is the legacy of Martin Luther King, Jr.? According to *Webster's New Collegiate Dictionary*, a legacy is defined as "something received from an ancestor, a predecessor, or from the past." As a working definition for this discourse, a legacy is defined as "something that has liberating and redemptive efficacy for its beneficiaries and impacts a significant population such as a nation."

A legacy can be negative or positive. Or, it can be both negative and positive, as is true of King's legacy. Sometimes it is the negative aspects rather than the positive aspects of a legacy that account for its permanency. Just because a legacy has a negative component, that does not mean that it should be ignored or considered to be of less value. Indeed, the positive component, as is true of King's legacy, may be of such that it, while not rendering the negative aspects as inconsequential, is so noble and of such redemptive value that its supremacy remains impeachable. Let us now consider the negative aspects of King's legacy. They are:

1. Nonviolence. King taught and required that his followers be nonviolent. One of the most noble commitments a person can make is to be responsible, to take the "responsibility vow." This should be done by a person at an early age. The responsible person answers the question, "What is the responsible thing to do in this specific situation?" The matter of self-preservation is taken seriously by the responsible person and he will defend himself against his destruction whenever it is in his power to do so. Think for a moment about people you know who have suffered needlessly, faced death or seen these things happen to people they care about because they are someone else who could have made a difference refused to be violent when it was clear that violence was the only remedy or viable option. There was not anything that happened during the Montgomery Bus Boycott or since that has caused me to change my mind about the need for me to reject the nonviolence approach that King advocated and asked bus protesters to embrace. Reality and love more than suggest that neither violence or nonviolence should be accepted as the single approach to be applied in living a creative and happy life. Standing in a responsibility posture, a person will employ violence or nonviolence in an endeavor to create the greatest good possible.

2. Passive Resistance. Although passive resistance appears to be closely related to nonviolence, it has its own specificity. Passive resistance runs counter to life, which is dynamic. That dynamism is expressed in a budding flower, heard when birds sing, and in the cry of a newborn baby. Passive resistance is a defensive tactic. And while there are times and circumstances when it is appropriate to be passive, even times when it is the prudent thing to do, there are many more times and circumstances which demand that we be assertive and even aggressive. This can be especially true when justice is being pursued. Translated, this means being on the offensive rather than the defensive, acting rather than reacting, and being a "doer" rather than a person or object "done to." Passive resistance suppresses or blocks

creativity and spontaneity, makes it difficult for a person to be peculiarly himself or capable of expressing his uniqueness. In order for a person to be in charge of himself, he has to reject passive resistance as a preferred behavioral pattern. Instead, he has to be assertive and express himself freely and forthrightly with the realization that he is a child of the Universe and has a right to be here on Planet Earth as much as any other creature or thing. I cannot recall many times when passive resistance helped us during the Montgomery bus boycott to accomplish our objective. However, I can think of many times, when its opposite, dynamic insistence, made a positive difference.

3. Dream Possessed. According to the news media and people who choose to ignore or minimize the significance of the meaning of the message King delivered, on August 23, 1963 at the Lincoln Memorial during the March on Washington, his speech is called the "I Have a Dream" speech. While it is true that toward the end of his speech he began at least five statements with "I have a dream," that was not the essential massage of his speech. In that speech, King informed and challenged white Americans to "Judge African Americans by the content of their character, not by the color of their skin." He said that the promissory note guaranteeing basic freedoms for all Americans, including black people, had come back marked "insufficient funds," and he asserted that "black people refuse to believe that the bank of justice is bankrupt." King called upon white Americans, ultimately the United States Government, to pay the long overdue payment that is due black Americans which for those of us who knew him best also knew that he meant the payment of reparations to black people for 244 years of enslavement of their ancestors. He challenged Americans to live out the American Creed set forth in the *Declaration of Independence* that says:

We hold these Truths to be self-evident, that all Men are created equal, that they are endowed by their Creator with certain unalienable Rights, that among these are Life, Liberty, and the Pursuit of Happiness.

Those who read King's speech with an open mind will readily understand that his speech was not a"dream speech," and should not be referred to as such. On that hot summer day, King called for a radical change that would eradicate racism, poverty and injustice in the American society. While it is also true that in his speech he said that his "I have a Dream" is rooted in the "American Dream," neither the "I Have a Dream" or the "American Dream" is a worthy goal for black folk to pursue. Freedom, justice and equality are not just American. They are desired and pursued by all human beings, not as a dream, but as a reality.

King was familiar with these words spoken by the Prophet Joel who said, "Your old men shall dream dreams, but your young men shall see visions" (Joel 2:28). King was a young man. Need I say more. And I have also heard him recite these words that are found in one of the wisdom books of the Bible that says, "Where there is no vision, the people perish." (Proverbs 29.18). And why this negative aspect of King's legacy is not fully of his making, but of those who interpret and present his message as the "I Have a Dream" mischaracterization of his essential message, it still must be considered a part of his legacy.

Now let us turn to the positive aspects of King's legacy. It bears repeating here: the positive components of one's legacy should not be rejected just because it co-exists with the negative components of his legacy.

1. Self-Respect. King believed that if a person had self-respect that he would also respect other people. He considered self-respect to be a moral attribute and an imperative for moral man.

Self-respect, propelled by love, enables a person to be his best. He admonished people to be the best. He would say, "sweep streets like Michelangelo painted and like Beethoven wrote music." To make this point he would sometimes quote this poem by Douglas Mallock:

If you can't be a pine on the top of the hill
Be a scrub in the valley—but be
the best little scrub by the side of the hill,
Be a bush if you can't be a tree.
If you can't be a highway just be a trail
If you can't be the sun be a star;
It isn't by size that you win or fail—
Be the best of whatever you are.

2. Confront Exploiters. King demonstrated that it is important to confront exploiters, and he felt that we should do it with the conviction that right will win. To him, confrontation meant that the challenger would carry out his own will in opposition to the will of the person or entity being challenged. Engaging in civil disobedience, protest marches, sit-ins and non-cooperation with evil were some of the ways King confronted exploiters. The Montgomery Bus Boycott is a classic example of non-cooperation with the "powers that be." The modus operandi employed in the bus boycott involved various methods and techniques that fit into the confrontative mystique.

3. Massive Desegregation. King's leadership contributed immensely in bringing about more integration in thirteen years than had been secured in all the years America had existed as a sovereign nation. Many of the inequities that Americans of African descent experienced before King's assault on the American system of segregation and racial discrimination have been eliminated or greatly reduced: in public transportation, employment and education. African Americans now have access to public facilities such as restaurants and hotels and open housing. They have the right to vote. These things can be attributed to King's leadership. Most significantly, his leadership helped to change the way laws would be supportive of black people. Simply put, they would make it possible for a black person to go to court and win when he had been the victim of racial discrimination. This is not to say that all the inequities and exclusions black people faced before King's assault on desegregation have disappeared. And since his death, some achievements made during his life have been lost or eroded. Many schools have become resegregated, affirmative action has been all but eliminated and black men, especially young black men, are currently being imprisoned on a scale not heretofore heard of, accounting for America holding the dubious distinction of being the world's number one jailer. But thanks to King's leadership, blacks are enjoying more of the opportunities and privileges of citizenship than ever before.

4. Practice Community. King taught that we can have "community or chaos, but not both." And he challenged humankind to practice community. Sometimes he called this way of being the

"practice of community" and at other times he called it the "Beloved Community." Emphasizing community he said, "Community is a relationship where people live together, respect each other and share themselves and their resources with each other." To illustrate the importance of community he would say, "We will live together or we will die separately." He observed that in community, "No link is any weaker than its strongest link." His answer to the question How do we know that we are practicing community? is, We know that we are practicing community when what we do contributes to creating and promoting oneness. For King, practicing community is a principle just the same as justice or love.

5. Spiritual Ultimacy. King believed that humans are spiritual beings and that spiritual power is the strongest power in the universe. He saw himself as a spiritual person and a Christian minister and he never ceased to maintain a faith-centeredness and a church-connectedness. Despite the pressure some people put on him and the attempts they made to get him to denounce or refuse to acknowledge his religious identity, he never forsook his role as a minister. He was challenged to be a civil rights leader, not a minister. King said that he did not have any conflict in being both a civil rights leader and a minister. For him they both were compatible. As a matter of fact, he drew heavily upon his minister self to enhance his civil rights leader self. And he was convinced not only that spiritual power is the strongest power in the universe, but that it was the only power that could effectively confront political power that is characteristically coercive and controlling, and as such it accounts for most of the injustice and human misery that afflicts society. On several occasions I heard him say that he was sent by God and that he was engaged in God's work. He never doubted that God would see him through his difficulties regardless of how insurmountable they may appear to be. I never heard King say anything to suggest or indicate that he believed that a non-Christian religious person was less than a Christian person. He would say "we are all God's children, including the non-professing religious person." There is much to indicate that every human being who has a soul is religious.

6. White Women Awakening. It was only after King led black people in effectively challenging the White Man to remove segregation barriers black people had faced did white women

171

become sufficiently motivated to engage in a struggle to secure equality for themselves. Apparently, they became convinced that if black people, men and women, could successfully challenge the white supremacy system that elevated white men over other people (their fathers, husbands and brothers), they could do likewise. To say that white women have kept a keen eye on black men, but also on black women, is no exaggeration. It was only after black men were granted the right to vote following the passage of the Fifteenth Amendment to the United States Constitution that was ratified on March 30, 1870, did white women engage in struggle to secure their right to vote which was granted fifty years later after the ratification of the Nineteenth Amendment to the United States Constitution on August 26, 1920. In the South, the Ku Klux Klan was organized to violently prevent black men from voting after the Fifteenth Amendment went into effect. Their tactics included lynching. Many states and federal governmental officials were either members of the Ku Klux Klan or felt powerless to resist Klansmen. The government abdicated its responsibility by failing to enforce the Fifteenth Amendment, something that should have been done even if it meant using the same methods to deal with the Ku Klux Klan that was used to deal with the South when Southern states attempted to secede from the union.

During the last thirty years, white women, using many of the tactics black people used in the fifties and sixties, have been highly successful in gaining access to opportunities that had been available only to white men. They have made phenomenal progress in achieving equality with white men and in narrowing the gap between themselves and their counterpart, meaning white men, more than it has been narrowed between black people and white people. Today, white women are doing nearly everything white men are doing, including fighting wars. This is a far cry from several generations earlier when their grandfathers and great-grandfathers put their grandmothers and great-grandmothers on pedestals and hailed them collectively the "weaker sex." That sounds like a contradiction.

7. Empowerment of Non-Black Minorities. Before King led blacks in protesting for their civil rights, many non-black minorities seemed to have been satisfied in just being treated by white people a little better than black people were treated by them. I have heard

some black people and some non-black minorities sum up the level of justice non-black minorities received using those very same words. Before King led the civil rights movement, Latinos voted in small numbers that could not be justified by the size of their population. They appeared to have been contented to let white people represent them, particularly in government, but also in non-governmental affairs. This was generally true with all non-black minorities, not just Latinos, in America, except for the Jews. It was as if non-black minorities believed that they were not entitled to the same rights, privileges, opportunities and responsibilities as white people. It was obvious that they did not enjoy the same citizenship rights as white people. Since Kings's civil rights crusade, Latinos, in particular, have made considerable progress. They now have real political power resulting in part from a significant increase in the number of registered voters they have and in the number of people they have elected to political offices. Indeed, they have become a political power to be reckoned with since King led the fight to secure voting rights for black people. The Fourteenth and Fifteenth Amendments to the United States Constitution gave them that right many years ago, but it was only after King raised their consciousness through his crusade to secure equal justice, under the law, for all did they register to vote in significant numbers. And significantly, Latinos have employed some of the same methods and strategies as King to gain greater access to the ballot box and other boxes that previously they did not have access to. However, they did not have to fight to open some of the doors to some boxes because King had fought to open them, not just to blacks but to Latinos. Clearly, Latinos are no longer just settling for what white leaders decide that is best for them, but are determining for themselves what actions they need to take in order to advance their own agenda in a society where white supremacy continues to reign as is evident in the amount of control white people have over non-white citizens and the vast percentage of the wealth they possess.

Among the other non-black minorities positively impacted by King's past civil rights leadership are the people of Asian descent, including Japanese; among them are the offsprings of Japanese who were placed in containment centers, American-style concentration camps, also called internment camps, during World War II, Chinese,

Filipinos, Koreans, Vietnamese, and Indians who are descendants of natives of India. Also included are other peoples of color who call America home, and black Americans from Africa whose ancestors did not cross the Atlantic on a slave ship during the Middle Passage but came by airplane, with few exceptions, since slavery was abolished in America. More importantly, however, than their mode of transportation is the fact that they came to America, of their own free-will, as free people, or, on their own accord. There are also Puerto Ricans and Cubans and it goes without saying, thanks to President John F. Kennedy's Cuban Policy, that Cubans are having a great impact on Florida. Both of these groups have applied King's direct action engagement strategy, particularly in New York City and Miami, respectively, to open doors that were previously closed to them. Haitians have also applied King's strategy on sea and land in demanding that they be treated like other immigrants, especially like white immigrants, fleeing their homelands in Europe to come to America. They, like some other Floridians, protested the treatment they received in Florida during the 2000 Presidential Election and complained that they were not given the kind of assistance at the polls that other non-English speaking groups received. And they joined with many others in asking that all the votes be counted, something the Supreme Court of the United States ruled against, notwithstanding, that the Florida Supreme Court had ruled that the votes should be counted. Many people believed, including those unfairly treated Haitians, that had the Florida Supreme Court ruling not been usurped by the U. S. Supreme Court and that the votes having been counted fairly Vice- President Albert Gore, not then Governor George W. Bush, would have become the forty-second President of the United States.

Native Americans, also called Indians, but never mind that nobody ever asked them their name, the most mistreated people in America, have on occasions applied King's approach of direct action with a touch of Sitting Bull acumen in seeking justice. King sometimes spoke of the mistreatment that Indians received at the hand of the white man and challenged white America to share the resources of this land in a more equitable way with the Indians.

Homosexuals, gays and lesbians, have come out of the closet since the civil rights years. It is apparent that they have employed some of the same tactics as King in their endeavor to be accepted. They have been involved in protest marches, most notably among them has been their gay and lesbians parades designed to declare their personhood visibility. Of course, in homophobia America just for gays and lesbians to show up or to admit their sexual orientation is a protest, just as it was for blacks before King's crusade. Just blacks' presence in certain arenas before King was intolerable to many white people. With regards to blacks, that has not entirely disappeared. Using King's approach to effect change homosexuals have gained what can be considered a tolerance, not acceptance, status in America. But they are continuing to work to achieve acceptance, as they employ King's methodology to accomplish their objectives.

Because homosexuals were politically active and the issue of their place in the military was being debated at the time William Jefferson Clinton first ran for President, he, sensing their clout, made a pledge to homosexuals that, if elected, he would give homosexual soldiers an acceptance status in the military. Early in his administration, most Republicans and some Democrats in the Congress advocated a homosexual-free military. President Clinton, after debating the matter, issued his four word military homosexual policy: "Don't ask, don't tell." Why the President deserved some credit for the brevity of his policy on homosexuals in the military, something that should be applied to many other governmental polices and, if such was the case, it would be more difficult to include in them a lot of the gobbledygook or non-sense that constitutes much of their content, this policy did not give recognition to the true identity or identities of homosexuals, or support them in their right to be themselves. Any governmental policy should encourage authenticity and truth. In that policy the words "Don't tell" should have been replaced with the words "Tell the truth." After the President issued that policy, Republicans who had charged him with not having a foreign policy could no longer say that he didn't have a policy on homosexuals in the military. During the Korean War, I was a soldier and there were homosexuals in every unit that I was assigned to. Other soldiers, except for the most naive among them, knew that homosexuals were present and accounted for at most roll calls. Let us not forget that during the war homosexuals, like heterosexuals, paid the ultimate price. Today some of them have the National Cemetery in Arlington, Virginia as their resting place. I must add that a policy for homosexuals and heterosexuals in the military that would have held the rank of general when compared with Clinton's policy that held, in my book, the rank of a private first-class or may be a private second-class, is "My business is my business and your business is your business."

Disabled people have also benefited from King's practices. They have engaged in direct action in seeking justice. Some AIDS victims and other disabled people have "acted up." That is what some white people accused King of doing. They included governmental officials and ministers. Among the ministers who felt that King acted up was Billy Graham. These status quo advocates wanted King to "act-down." Of course, they preferred that he not act at all, particularly if it meant seeking to change the status quo. King's letter from a Birmingham jail was his response to clergymen's criticism of his leadership. Prior to going to jail in Birmingham, some white clergymen, after castigating and lampooning him, urged him to withdraw from demonstrations. In his letter from the Birmingham jail he said, "We cannot be satisfied...we can never be satisfied...we cannot be satisfied as long as a Negro in Mississippi cannot vote and a Negro in New York believes he has nothing for which to vote." Then in his most scathing accusations of a reprimanding nature and confession he said:

> *I must make two honest confessions to you, my Christian and Jewish brothers. First, I must confess that over the last few years I have been gravely disappointed with the white moderate. I have almost reached the regrettable conclusion that the Negro's great stumbling block is not the White Citizen's Council-er or the Ku Klux Klanner, but the white moderate who is more devoted to "order" than to justice, who prefers a negative peace which is the absence of tension to a positive peace which is the presence of justice, who constantly says, "I agree with you in the goal you seek, but I can't agree with your methods of direct action," who paternalistically believe that he can set the timetable for another man's freedom.*

I predict that the next two groups that will employ King's

philosophy and practices will be the homeless and prisoners. Of course, some homeless people have been sent to prison for no other reason than they were homeless. While they have shown their colors, so to speak, with most of them being black or brown and, of course, poor, they have not applied the tactics King used to advance their civil rights agenda. What do you think would happen if a large number, say fifty percent, of the homeless decided to show up for prison? Do you think the system would make one clean sweep of the homeless as some cities have insisted on doing to rid their cities of homeless people and forcing them to go to another city or remanding them to a restricted part of their cities? What would happen if the prisoners decided that they would no longer accept their prisoner status which, among other things, would mean that they would refuse to render free labor that enriches people who have no claim on being compensated by prisoners.

Today there are approximately three million people in American prisons and jails and another six million on probation or kept under the "criminal-eyed" surveillance of the American justice system which, in reality, for many, is as much an injustice system as it is a justice system. Nearly half of the prisoners are black, many of them young black men, even though blacks constitute only eleven percent of the United States population. Even ex-prisoners, so-called felons, are often denied their rights, including the right to vote, to own a gun, and to work on a decent job after completing their sentences. States in the South and those elsewhere that have large black populations are the states that have the most punitive "after serving prison time" laws. It would seem that in any sane and humane society a helping hand would be extended to those who have fallen and that they would be encouraged to become productive citizens. But that is not the case in America. It is time for people from all walks of life to realize that a person is more than his past or the acts that he has committed. He is his present, his problems, his growth and the possibilities, including the possibility that he can soar to higher heights. The main reason so many people are sent to and kept in prisons is because it is economically profitable. Judges, prosecuting attorneys, security guards and many other people owe their financial well-being to the justice system, not least being to prisoners. If it were not for prisoners, many judges would not be judging. What do you think they would be doing? After all, a number of them were political appointees. Of course, unemployment is not among the possibilities, or is it? Unfortunately, prisoners do not realize how much power they possess. When they come to that realization they will use the tactics King employed to gain justice. I believe that the time is swiftly approaching when they will fight for their own freedom. The greatest power any person has is soul-power. This is what King believed. Soul-power can be used to enable a person to transcend his predicament. Saint Ambrose observed that "A wise man, though he be a slave, is at liberty." To paraphrase one can say, "A spiritual aware person, though in prison, is free." All Americans who believe in "justice for all" or justice for themselves have a responsibility to join in a crusade aimed at radically reforming the prison system just as all right thinking Americans had a responsibility during King's crusade days to join in opposing segregation and racial discrimination. Sometimes we hear people say, "America is the greatest nation in the world." We never ask, "for whom?" Well, to repeat, for a certainty, "America is the world's largest jailer." And, it may be well for those who proudly declare that "America is the greatest nation in the world," to say with a sense of turpitude, "America is the "world's largest jailer."

Before making a closing statement, I want to state that even though I have talked about King in such a way that the reader might get the impression that King single-handedly led the civil rights movement, that was not the case, nor do I want to infer that misunderstanding. King would be the first person to give a lot of people credit for the success of the Montgomery Bus Boycott and other civil-rights feats and advances that followed. He realized, as I do, that there were other leaders and people who made it possible for him to provide the leadership that would advance the civil rights agenda and effect social change. Indeed, if he had not known that before the bus boycott, he certainly learned that during the boycott that he led effectively. Even some leaders and groups that opposed King's leadership were important in that regard. They, too, contributed to opening more doors of opportunity for black people. Their roles were vital in assisting King, even when they appeared to be in opposition to him. They can be accredited, to a great degree, with keeping King on the right tracks.

These groups and personalities included, but were not limited to, the Student Nonviolent Coordinating Committee, Malcolm X and the Black Power Warrior Stokely Carmichael. A truth that is not always apparent is that King's black opponents helped to advance the civil rights movement and make it a success. The Malcolm X "by any means necessary" and Carmichael's "Black Power" approaches actually caused white controllers, including the government, to make concessions and overtures to King that would not have happened had it not been for their engagements. There is no doubt in my mind that in the long run their actions brought some benefits, including the right to vote to black people in the South sooner than they would have become available to them had they not, in certain ways, opposed King or his tactics. In fact, their actions helped to make for fewer black casualties. Then there were other groups, the most notable among them were the Congress of Racial Equality and the NAACP and their leaders, James Farmer and Roy Wilkins, respectively. It remains, however, that King was not only the most prominent leader of the civil rights movement, but he contributed more to its success than anyone else and, perhaps, it was because he had the greatest capacity to do more. Jesus spoke to this when he said, "For unto whomsoever much is given, of him shall be much required" (Luke 12:48). All people are not endowed with the same gifts or given the same amount of talents quality-wise or quantity-wise.

And now the end is near. The evening shadows appear. It is the day before King's death. He had come to Memphis to participate in a second march that was aimed at securing justice for garbage workers. He had not been at the first march that occurred a week earlier when there was violence. He applauded what the protesters were doing to secure justice but he wanted nonviolence to prevail. The local leaders, including Rev. James Lawson, pastor of a local church, who for several years had been King's chief nonviolent trainer, asked him to come to Memphis and participate in the march and assist them in obtaining justice.

On that very night, King delivered his last public message at the Church of God in Christ's Mason Temple. He told his audience about the bomb threat on his plane that morning and rumors that some people in Memphis were threatening him, too. In his final public message, speaking prophetically and seemingly with clairvoyance and a premonition he said:

Well, I don't know what will happen now. We've got some difficult days ahead. But it really doesn't matter with me now, because I've been to the mountaintop. And I don't mind. Like anybody, I would like to live a long life. Longevity has its place. But I'm not concerned about that now. I just want to do God's will. And He's allowed me to go up to the mountain, and I've looked over, and I've seen the promised land. I may not get there with you. But I want you to know tonight, that we, as a people will get to the promised land. And so I'm happy tonight. I'm not worried about anything. I'm not fearing any man. Mine eyes have seen the glory of the coming of the Lord.

The legacy of King is a gift for humanity and is of great value. It has been paid for sacrificially. In his struggle for justice he gave his life or, more correctly, it was taken away from him because of what he stood for. His legacy is efficacious and redemptive. Better than anyone except Jesus, he motivated and encouraged people in a way that they had not experienced in modern times if, indeed before, to take seriously the possibility and probability that they can create brotherhood, the Beloved Community, and a societal transformation. Because of King many more people than before have become involved in transforming society. They have and continue to accept the challenge he made when he urged them to improve upon what their parents and forefathers had done and not just settle for or resign to limiting themselves to their forefather's achievements. The abuse of black people was one of the wrongs their parents and forefathers had committed that he inspired them to address, rather than to ignore or refuse to respond to positively and humanely. He challenged them to never agree that their foreparents were right in supporting slavery and practicing racial discrimination. In response to King's demonstration of caring about those who are unjustly treated, many young people broke with their parents, with tradition and rejected white supremacy. They responded to King's admonition which was the same call that the Prophet Amos made when he said, "But let justice run down like waters, and righteousness like an overflowing stream" (Amos 5:24). Because of King, people began to feel and demonstrate that individually or collectively they could make a difference.

My prayer and charge, and it is a mandate as well, to readers of this volume and to those they share this message with is: resolve to consciously embrace the "Legacy of Martin Luther King, Jr." with the awareness that each individual has to work out his own personal salvation for himself in fear and trembling, but that we can help one another to find meaning, and in doing this we become better and we help to create a better world. Both we and the world are still in the making. These are things King realized and endeavored to assist others in knowing, and knowing to commit to do good and work for the creation of a just society.

King is one of the few extraordinarily gifted and distinguished Masters of all human existence who have kept alive the "Paradise Regained" hope that is rooted in the divine promise that we can live in a just society. This is our inheritance. From eternity King speaks to our salient spirits saying, "Claim your inheritance!" Dare we, beneficiaries of his legacy, forget to treasure it and to transmit it to our children and teach them to pass it on to their children so that it will live in perpetuity.

ACKNOWLEDGMENTS

I acknowledge with gratitude my infinite debt to the Nameless One, called by many names, the Giver of Life, Who gave me a memory that enabled me to remember things that occurred more than two score years ago, in many instances, as if they had happened yesterday.

I acknowledge with gratitude Reverend A. W. Wilson, pastor of the Holt Street Baptist Church in Montgomery, where the first mass meeting of the bus boycott was held, Rosa Parks who refused to give up her seat on a bus to allow a white man to be seated at a time when African Americans were willing and ready to make a positive response to the injustice that they had experienced as bus riders, Martin Luther King, Jr., whose extraordinary leadership made it possible for the 382-day long bus boycott to end with desegregation of Montgomery buses and Ralph David Abernathy, his right hand lieutenant and trusted companion.

I acknowledge with gratitude more than twenty persons, all participants in the bus boycott, who, decades after that historical event, shared their personal knowledge with me. Without their cooperation I would have not been able to write this book.

I acknowledge with gratitude the works of David J. Garrow, Taylor Branch and Clayborne Carson on the bus boycott. It is my opinion that they have written, to date, the best books available on the subject.

I acknowledge with gratitude E. D. Nixon for his collaboration with me over a period of nearly thirty years during and after the bus boycott. He encouraged me to write this book and in fidelity I dedicate this book to him.

INDEX

Abernathy, Ralph David, 5, 12, 36, 41-46, 50-52, 55, 61-64, 69, 72-73, 77, 85-94, 99-101, 104, 108, 114, 122, 128, 130-135, 157, 160, 183

AIDS, 176

Alabama State College, 16, 20-29, 34-35, 40, 47, 49, 64, 73, 87, 127-128, 147, 149

Alabama Christian Movement for Human Rights, 127

Alabama Council on Human Relations, 54

Alabama Journal, 37

Alabama Negro Baptist Center, 59

Alabama Register of Landmarks, 33

Alabama Historical Commission, 33

Alford, W. F.,

American Christian Freedom Society,

American Dream,

American of African Descent,

Amos,

Anti-boycott law,

"Arelia S. Browder v. William A. Gayle,"

Army,

Awakening,

Azbell, Joe,

Ball, Fred,

Bagley, James H.,

Baltaxe, George,

Baptist Ministers' Conference,

Baskin, Inez J.,

Bear, Joe,

Bell, E. D.,

Bell Street Baptist Church,

Bennett, L. Roy,
Beloved Community,
Bethel Baptist Church,
Billingsley, Orzell,
Birmingham Jail,
Black, Hugo, L.,
Black Power,
Black Radio Station,
Blair, P. M.,
Blake, J. D.,
Bonner, J. W.,
Branch, Taylor,
Brewer, Juanita,
Browder, Aurelia, S.,
Brownell, Herbert,
"Brown v. Board of Education of Topeka",
Burks, Mary Fair,
Bush, George, W.,
Butler, Bertha,
Butler, Mack Sim,

Carmichael, Stokely,
Carr, Leanord G.,
Car Pool,
Carson, Clayborne,
Carter, Eugene,
Carter, Robert L.,
Christian Principles,
Christmas Spirit,
Church Bombings,
Church of God in Christ Mason Temple,
Citizens Club,
Civil Rights Congress,
Civil Rights Movement,
Class-consciousness,
Cleveland, M. C.,
Clinton, William Jefferson,
Club-Twenty-one,

Race Relations,
Racism,
Randolph, A. Philip,
Rawls, Louis,
Ray, James Earl,
Ray, Sandy,
Recommendations,
Reconstruction Committee for Bombed Churches,
Reddick, L. D.,
Redemption,
Reese, Jeanetta,
Religion,
Reparations,
Resolutions Committee,
Retaliation,
Retraction,
Rice, Doc C.,
Richardson, Harry V.,
Rives, Richard,
Robeson, Paul,
Robinson, Jo. Ann,
Rogers, T. Y.,
Rosenberg, Ethel,
Rosenberg, Julius,
Roosevelt, Franklin, D.,
Rowan, Carl T.,
Ruppenthal, G. J.,
Rustin Bayard,

Salient Spirits,
Salvation,
Scott, Dred,
Scott, John B.,
Seay, S. S.,
Segregation,
Self-Defense,
Self-Respect, Self-Preservation, Self-Validation,
Sellers, Clyde,

Voters Registration,

Waller, Luther H.,
Washington, Booker T.,
White Citizens Council
White Supremacy,
Wilkins, Roy,
Williams, Roscoe,
Wilson, A. W.,
Witness,
Women's Political Council,

YMCA,
Young, Ronald R,